EUROPEAN ECONOMIC AND POLITICAL ISSUES

ECONOMIC CRISIS IN THE EUROZONE

OVERVIEW, OUTLOOK AND ANALYSES

European Economic and Political Issues

Additional books in this series can be found on Nova's website under the Series tab.

Additional e-books in this series can be found on Nova's website under the e-books tab.

Global Economic Studies

Additional books in this series can be found on Nova's website under the Series tab.

Additional e-books in this series can be found on Nova's website under the e-books tab.

EUROPEAN ECONOMIC AND POLITICAL ISSUES

ECONOMIC CRISIS IN THE EUROZONE

OVERVIEW, OUTLOOK AND ANALYSES

ELLEN F. YOUNG
AND
TYE D. MURPHY
EDITORS

nova publishers
New York

For permission to use material from this book please contact us:
Telephone 631-231-7269; Fax 631-231-8175
Web Site: http://www.novapublishers.com

LIBRARY OF CONGRESS CATALOGING-IN-PUBLICATION DATA

ISBN: 978-1-62081-788-9

Published by Nova Science Publishers, Inc. † New York

Contents

Preface		**vii**
Chapter 1	The Eurozone Crisis: Overview and Issues for Congress *Rebecca M. Nelson, Paul Belkin, Derek E. Mix and Martin A. Weiss*	**1**
Chapter 2	Statement of Treasury Secretary Tim Geithner. Hearing on "Europe's Sovereign Debt Crisis: Causes, Consequences for the United States and Lessons Learned"	**29**
Chapter 3	Statement of Federal Reserve Chairman Ben Bernanke. Hearing on "Europe's Sovereign Debt Crisis: Causes, Consequences for the United States and Lessons Learned"	**35**
Chapter 4	Statement of C. Fred Bergsten Director, Peterson Institute for International Economics. Hearing on "Outlook for the Eurozone"	**41**
Chapter 5	Statement of Simon Johnson. Hearing on "Outlook for the Eurozone"	**61**
Chapter 6	Statement of Adam Lerrick, Scholar from the American Enterprise Institute. Hearing on "Outlook for the Eurozone"	**79**

Chapter 7 Testimony of Lael Brainard, Under Secretary for International Affairs. Hearing on "Examining the European Debt Crisis and its Implications" **83**

Chapter 8 Testimony of Steven B. Kamin, Director of International Finance Division. Hearing on "Examining the European Debt Crisis and its Implications" **89**

Chapter 9 Testimony of Bert Ely. Hearing on "What the Euro Crisis Means for Taxpayers and the U.S. Economy, Part 1" **95**

Chapter 10 Testimony of Jacob Funk Kirkegaard. Hearing on "The European Debt Crisis: Strategic Implications for the Transatlantic Alliance" **105**

Index **125**

PREFACE

What started as a debt crisis in Greece in late 2009 has evolved into a broader economic crisis in the Eurozone that threatens economic stability in Europe and beyond. Many analysts consider the Eurozone crisis to be the biggest threat to the global economy, and some Members of Congress have expressed concern about the possible effects on the U.S. economic recovery. Analysts and investors are concerned that some Eurozone governments could default on their debt in a disorderly fashion; vulnerabilities in the European banking sector could trigger broad financial turmoil; the Eurozone could enter a protracted economic recession; and one or more countries could leave the Eurozone. The crisis has tested the solidarity of European Union (EU) member states and strained the capacity of EU leadership and institutional structures. This book provides a brief analysis of the Eurozone crisis and issues of particular congressional interest.

Chapter 1 – What started as a debt crisis in Greece in late 2009 has evolved into a broader economic crisis in the Eurozone that threatens economic stability in Europe and beyond. Some analysts view the Eurozone crisis as the biggest potential threat to the U.S. economic recovery. The Eurozone faces at least four major, and related, economic challenges. These challenges include: 1) high debt levels and public deficits in some Eurozone countries; 2) weaknesses in the European banking system; 3) economic recession and high unemployment in some Eurozone countries; and 4) persistent trade imbalances within the Eurozone.

European leaders have undertaken several rounds of unprecedented policy measures to resolve the crisis. Key policy measures focus on: austerity measures and structural and economic reforms in countries facing severe market pressure, including Greece, Ireland, Italy, Portugal, and Spain (often referred to as the Eurozone "periphery"); financial assistance from other Eurozone governments and the IMF to Greece, Ireland, and Portugal; plans for debt restructuring in Greece; European Central Bank (ECB) liquidity support to private banks and purchases of sovereign bonds on secondary markets; and a commitment by most countries in the European Union (EU) to balance national budgets, the so-called "fiscal compact."

Although the ECB's infusion of cash into the banking system in December 2011 and February 2012 through long-term refinancing operations appears to have calmed markets, significant risks and policy questions remain. Particular concerns center on how to restore growth in the Eurozone periphery amidst often unpopular austerity reforms; how to put Greece's debt on a sustainable path; and how to correct trade imbalances in the Eurozone. More broadly, there are questions about the impact of the crisis on the future of the Eurozone. Some economists are optimistic that ultimately the European leaders and institutions will do whatever is necessary to keep the Eurozone from collapsing, and that the Eurozone will emerge from the crisis stronger and more integrated. Others view a broader financial crisis triggered by a disorderly default or exit by one or more countries from the Eurozone as a real possibility.

Chapter 2 – This is Statement of Treasury Secretary Tim Geithner before the House Committee on Oversight and Government Reform, Hearing on "Europe's Sovereign Debt Crisis: Causes, Consequences for the United States and Lessons Learned".

Chapter 3 – This is Statement of Federal Reserve Chairman Ben Bernanke before the House Committee on Oversight and Government Reform, Hearing on "Europe's Sovereign Debt Crisis: Causes, Consequences for the United States and Lessons Learned".

Chapter 4 – This is Statement of C. Fred Bergsten before the Senate Budget Committee, Hearing on "Outlook for the Eurozone".

Chapter 5 – This is Statement of Simon Johnson before the Senate Budget Committee, Hearing on "Outlook for the Eurozone".

Chapter 6 – This is Statement of Adam Lerrick, Scholar from the American Enterprise Institute before the Senate Budget Committee, Hearing on "Outlook for the Eurozone".

Chapter 7 – This is Testimony of Lael Brainard, Under Secretary for International Affairs, U.S. Treasury Department, before the Senate Banking Committee, Hearing on "Examining the European Debt Crisis and its Implications".

Chapter 8 – This is Testimony of Steven B. Kamin, Director of International Finance Division, Board of Governors of the Federal Reserve System before the Senate Banking Committee, Hearing on "Examining the European Debt Crisis and its Implications".

Chapter 9 – This is Testimony of Bert Ely before the House Committee on Oversight and Government Reform, Hearing on "What the Euro Crisis Means for Taxpayers and the U.S. Economy, Part 1".

Chapter 10 - This is Testimony of Jacob Funk Kirkegaard before the Senate Foreign Relations Committee, Hearing on "The European Debt Crisis: Strategic Implications for the Transatlantic Alliance".

In: Economic Crisis in the Eurozone ISBN: 978-1-62081-788-9
Editors: E. F. Young and T. D. Murphy

Chapter 1

THE EUROZONE CRISIS: OVERVIEW AND ISSUES FOR CONGRESS*

Rebecca M. Nelson, Paul Belkin, Derek E. Mix and Martin A. Weiss

SUMMARY

What started as a debt crisis in Greece in late 2009 has evolved into a broader economic crisis in the Eurozone that threatens economic stability in Europe and beyond. Some analysts view the Eurozone crisis as the biggest potential threat to the U.S. economic recovery. The Eurozone faces at least four major, and related, economic challenges. These challenges include: 1) high debt levels and public deficits in some Eurozone countries; 2) weaknesses in the European banking system; 3) economic recession and high unemployment in some Eurozone countries; and 4) persistent trade imbalances within the Eurozone.

European leaders have undertaken several rounds of unprecedented policy measures to resolve the crisis. Key policy measures focus on: austerity measures and structural and economic reforms in countries facing severe market pressure, including Greece, Ireland, Italy, Portugal, and Spain (often referred to as the Eurozone "periphery"); financial assistance from other

* This is an edited, reformatted and augmented version of the Congressional Research Service Publication, CRS Report for Congress R42377, dated February 29, 2012.

Eurozone governments and the IMF to Greece, Ireland, and Portugal; plans for debt restructuring in Greece; European Central Bank (ECB) liquidity support to private banks and purchases of sovereign bonds on secondary markets; and a commitment by most countries in the European Union (EU) to balance national budgets, the so-called "fiscal compact."

Although the ECB's infusion of cash into the banking system in December 2011 and February 2012 through long-term refinancing operations appears to have calmed markets, significant risks and policy questions remain. Particular concerns center on how to restore growth in the Eurozone periphery amidst often unpopular austerity reforms; how to put Greece's debt on a sustainable path; and how to correct trade imbalances in the Eurozone. More broadly, there are questions about the impact of the crisis on the future of the Eurozone. Some economists are optimistic that ultimately the European leaders and institutions will do whatever is necessary to keep the Eurozone from collapsing, and that the Eurozone will emerge from the crisis stronger and more integrated. Others view a broader financial crisis triggered by a disorderly default or exit by one or more countries from the Eurozone as a real possibility.

Issues for Congress

Impact on the U.S. Economy: The United States and Europe share the largest bilateral economic relationship in the world, and there are concerns about the exposure of U.S. financial institutions to Europe and U.S. exports to Europe. Treasury officials have emphasized that U.S. exposure to the Eurozone countries under the most market pressure is small but that U.S. exposure to Europe as a whole is significant. To date, it is not clear that U.S.-EU trade flows have contracted, although risks may remain.

IMF Involvement: Some Members of Congress are concerned about IMF involvement in the Eurozone crisis. In 2010, Congress passed legislation to limit IMF support for advanced economies (P.L. 111-203). In the 112th Congress, legislation has been introduced in the House and the Senate to rescind some U.S. contributions to the IMF (for example, H.R. 2313; S.Amdt. 501), but at present has not become law. The Treasury Department has indicated that the United States will not contribute additional funds to the IMF.

U.S.-European Cooperation: The United States looks to Europe for partnership in addressing a wide range of global challenges. Some analysts and U.S. and European officials have expressed concern that the crisis could turn the EU's focus more inward and exacerbate a long-standing downward trend in European defense spending.

INTRODUCTION

Over the past two years, the Eurozone has grappled with a sovereign debt crisis that threatens economic stability in Europe and beyond.[1] Analysts and investors are concerned that some Eurozone governments could default on their debt in a disorderly fashion;[2] vulnerabilities in the European banking sector could trigger broad financial turmoil; the Eurozone could enter a protracted economic recession; and one or more countries could leave the Eurozone.

The crisis has tested the solidarity of European Union (EU) member states and strained the capacity of EU leadership and institutional structures. Key European leaders have repeatedly vowed to take all necessary measures to protect the euro, which they view as the cornerstone of the European integration project.[3] They have held numerous summits and announced several rounds of policy measures to try to resolve the crisis. However, analysts have routinely criticized these measures as insufficient, and questions about economic, financial, and political stability in the Eurozone persist. The Obama Administration has repeatedly called for swift and robust European responses—specifically advocating more substantial financial assistance be made available to struggling economies. It has found, however, that it may have limited ability to affect European policy decisions.

Many analysts consider the Eurozone crisis to be the biggest threat to the global economy,[4] and some Members of Congress have expressed concern about the possible effects on the U.S. economy. Some Members have also raised questions about the appropriate role of the International Monetary Fund (IMF) in the crisis, particularly in light of the fact that the United States is the Fund's largest shareholder. Implications for future U.S.-EU cooperation on foreign policy issues more broadly is also a concern. Committees in both the House and the Senate have held hearings on the crisis and issues relating to possible U.S. exposure and U.S. policy responses.[5]

ECONOMIC PROBLEMS IN THE EUROZONE

The current Eurozone crisis has been unfolding since late 2009, when a new Greek government revealed that previous Greek governments had been underreporting the budget deficit. The crisis subsequently spread to Ireland and Portugal, while raising concerns about Italy, Spain, the European banking system, and more fundamental imbalances within the Eurozone.

Currently, the Eurozone is facing at least four major, and related, economic challenges:

First, concerns persist about high levels of public debt in some Eurozone countries, often referred to as the "periphery," and whether these countries will default on their debt.[6] Debt levels in some countries in the Eurozone periphery rose after they joined the Eurozone over a decade ago,[7] and the global financial crisis of 2008-2009 further strained public finances (see **Figure 1** and **Figure 2**). Three Eurozone governments—Greece, followed by Ireland and subsequently Portugal—have had to borrow money from other Eurozone governments and the IMF in order to avoid defaulting on their debt. Even with this assistance, the Greek government is currently negotiating "haircuts" (losses) on bonds held by private creditors, and there is speculation that Portugal will also have to restructure its debt.[8]

Investors have become increasingly nervous about high debt levels in Italy and rising debt levels in Spain, much larger economies, and they have started demanding higher interest rates for buying and holding Italian and Spanish bonds. As the Spanish and Italian governments have rolled over their debt at these higher interest rates, their debt levels have risen further, and questions have emerged about the sustainability of public debt in these countries. A disorderly default by a Eurozone country could trigger a broader financial crisis. Possible contagion of the crisis to Italy is a particular concern; Italian government debt is forecasted to be €2.1 trillion (about $2.8 billion)[9] in 2012, greater than that of Spain, Portugal, Greece, and Ireland combined, and four times larger than Europe's financial assistance funds (see "Major European Policy Responses").[10]

Second, weaknesses in the Eurozone's banking system are compounding concerns about public debt levels. Most urgently, ongoing concerns about the crisis have triggered capital flight from banks in some Eurozone countries, and some banks are reportedly finding it difficult to borrow in private capital markets.[11] More broadly, European banks are believed to be the largest holders of Eurozone government bonds, but many analysts argue that European banks do not have sufficient capital to absorb losses on their holdings of sovereign bonds should one or more Eurozone governments default. In December 2011, the European Banking Authority (EBA) estimated that European banks need €114.5 billion (about $152 billion) in additional capital in order to withstand a range of shocks and still maintain adequate capital.[12] The EBA is currently reviewing plans from European financial institutions to restore their capital positions by the end of June 2012,[13] and some analysts fear that banks will improve their capital positions by reducing lending, exacerbating the credit crunch in Europe and, in turn, contributing to an economic recession.

Third, there are concerns about the lack of growth and high unemployment in the Eurozone, particularly among the Eurozone periphery. In January 2012, the IMF downgraded its growth forecast for the Eurozone, from growing by 1.1% in 2012 to contracting by 0.5%.[14] The Organization for Economic Cooperation and Development (OECD) forecasts that the economies of Greece, Portugal, and Italy will contract in 2012. Unemployment is particularly high in the Eurozone periphery, forecasted to be 18.5% in Greece and 22.9% in Spain in 2012 (see Figure 4).[15] Youth unemployment is significantly higher, approaching 50% in Greece and Spain.[16] Slow growth or recession makes it hard for countries to grow out of their debt, and exacerbates debt-to-GDP ratios. The crisis is also adversely impacting growth in traditionally stronger Eurozone economies, with the IMF forecasting that growth in Germany will drop from 3.0% of GDP in 2011 to 0.3% in 2012, and drop from 1.6% in 2011 to 0.2% in France in 2012.

Fourth, persistent trade imbalances have developed within the Eurozone over the past decade, and some argue that these imbalances make the Eurozone more vulnerable to financial crises. Core countries in the Eurozone, including Germany, have actively pursued policies, such as wage restraint, aimed at increasing economic competitiveness by keeping production costs low and bolstering exports. Production costs in the Eurozone periphery tend to be higher, due to a number of structural issues such as rigid labor markets, generous pension programs, and barriers to economic competition. As a result, Eurozone core countries tend to run trade surpluses with the Eurozone periphery, and, by the same token, the periphery countries tend to run trade deficits with the core countries. These trade imbalances have been associated with a corresponding trend of the Eurozone's stronger economies lending to weaker economies, with the governments or private sectors in the Eurozone periphery building up sizeable debts. Eurozone countries have found it difficult to correct these trade imbalances, because membership in the Eurozone takes away a key adjustment mechanism—the exchange rate—for correcting trade imbalances. Many economists believe that the buildup of high levels of debt and persistent trade imbalances can be unstable, and increase vulnerability to confidence shocks in financial markets.

More broadly, the crisis has exposed problems in the structure of the Eurozone, which many economists have long debated. The Eurozone has a common monetary policy and currency, without creating a fiscal union, but does not have a centralized budget authority or system of fiscal transfers across members. Possibly, under a tight fiscal union, a central budget authority could control spending in different Eurozone member states, and use fiscal transfers to smooth out asymmetric shocks within the Eurozone.

Major European Policy Responses

Over the past two years, the policy response in Europe has been consistently criticized as delivering too little, too late. Deep disagreements among Germany, France, and the European Central Bank (ECB) over the appropriate response, as well as what is widely viewed as a slow and complex EU policy-making process are seen as having exacerbated anxiety in markets throughout the crisis. Additionally, domestic political obstacles have hindered more significant policy responses. Austerity measures have provoked a number of sustained, large scale protests across Europe, and the crisis contributed to the fall of governments in Greece, Ireland, Italy, Portugal, Spain, and Slovenia. Leaders in some of the Eurozone core countries have had to overcome considerable political resistance to providing financial support to countries in trouble, with critics opposed to the idea of rescuing countries that, in their view, did not exercise adequate budget discipline.

European leaders and institutions have implemented a number of unprecedented policy measures to try to stop, or at least contain, the crisis over the past two years. Some of the key measures include:

Financial Assistance from other Eurozone governments and the IMF. The cornerstone of the EU response has been to create new crisis lending facilities that can provide financial support to governments and financial institutions in the Eurozone that are under market pressure. Details of these funds have evolved over time, but the main rescue fund currently in operation is the European Financial Stability Facility (EFSF). It has a lending capacity of €440 billion (about $584 billion) and its resources can currently be used to provide assistance to governments, finance bank recapitalization, or purchase government bonds on secondary markets. The EFSF is a temporary, three-year facility, expected to be replaced by a permanent rescue fund, the European Stabilization Mechanism (ESM) in 2013. The EFSF and ESM will overlap in 2012, during which time the total ceiling on EFSF/ESM lending will be raised to €500 billion (about $664 billion), although this ceiling will be reassessed in March 2012. Currently, the EFSF is providing financial assistance, in conjunction with the IMF, to Ireland and Portugal. Greece is also receiving financial assistance from the IMF and other Eurozone governments, but since its program was devised before the creation of the EFSF, Eurozone government support to Greece takes the form of separate bilateral loans from other governments. A second financial assistance package to Greece has been announced, and is to be funded by the EFSF. For more details about these packages, see **Table 1**.

Austerity Programs and Structural Reforms. European and IMF financial assistance comes with strings attached. European and IMF financial assistance to Greece, Ireland, and Portugal has been disbursed to the countries in phases, only after a committee with representatives from the IMF, the European Commission, and the ECB determined that sufficient progress on austerity and structural reforms had been made. In both Greece and Portugal, for example, far-reaching spending cuts and targeted tax increases have reduced government budget deficits significantly over the past two years. However, both economies continue to contract, making it increasingly difficult to meet agreed-upon debt-reduction targets. Both countries have also begun to reform their pension systems and bring more flexibility to what remain rigid labor markets, but observers note that progress has at times been slow and question how long political support for the measures will continue. Of the three countries receiving financial assistance, Ireland is considered to have made the most progress. Nonetheless, observers caution that public opposition to the EU's "fiscal compact" (see below on European economic governance reforms) could impede success.

Governments in Italy and Spain have also undertaken far-reaching austerity measures and reforms in an effort to re-gain market confidence and build competitiveness. The Spanish government, which passed a balanced budget amendment in 2011, has pledged to bring its budget deficit to 3% of GDP by 2013, and has proposed a series of labor-market reforms that would result in a decline in real wages. The Italian government has announced similar initiatives, pledging, among other things, to balance its budget by 2013. Such reforms have been politically difficult to implement, provoking public protests and may have contributed to changes in government in some Eurozone countries.

Losses on Greek Bonds. The Greek government is currently negotiating with private investors on the size of voluntary "haircuts" on Greek bonds. If the losses are not accepted voluntarily, but imposed on private bondholders, payment on credit default swap (CD S) contracts on Greek bonds are expected to be triggered, which some fear could cause instability in financial markets.[17] However, even if the "haircuts" are accepted by private bond holders, the stated goal is to reduce Greece's debt level to only 120% of GDP by 2020,[18] which some economists fear would still be too high to be sustainable. European leaders have publicly ruled out debt restructuring (often called "private sector involvement") for other Eurozone countries.

ECB Support. The ECB significantly increased its role in the crisis response in December 2011, when it introduced long-term refinancing operations (LTRO). The LTRO resulted in loans to more than 500 Eurozone banks, totaling €489 billion (about $649 billion), and is the biggest infusion of cash into the banking system since the euro was introduced. The ECB launched a second round of LTRO in February 2012, which was even bigger, totaling an additional €530 billion (about $ 704 billion) and had more than 800 banks participating. The LTRO aim to address the liquidity crunch in the Eurozone banking system and to encourage banks to continue buying Spanish and Italian government bonds.[19]

Previously, in May 2010, the ECB began buying government bonds on secondary markets for the first time in an attempt to stabilize bond yields, and the ECB is now believed to be the biggest holder of Greek bonds.[20] The ECB has also provided unusual flexibility in its short-term refinancing operations throughout the crisis, in particular by agreeing to accept securities, including government bonds, with lower credit ratings on collateral in its refinancing operations than it would have under normal circumstances.

European Governance Reforms. In December 2011, EU leaders announced the creation of a new fiscal compact. The primary focus of the fiscal compact is an agreement that government budgets should be balanced or in surplus, and that constitutions should be amended to reflect this rule. The compact would also strengthen the enforcement of EU rules related to debt levels and budget deficits, including by allowing European authorities to launch infringement proceedings at the EU Court of Justice against governments in breach of the rules. In January 2012, leaders of 25 of the EU's 27 member states concluded a draft text on the agreement, but it will still need to be adopted at the national level, and may require referendums in some countries.

The UK has announced it would not participate after it was unable to secure safeguards regarding financial supervision and regulation, and the Czech Republic did likewise because it did not have the necessary mandate from its parliament. In late 2011, the EU also adopted legislation, dubbed the "European Semester," containing additional reforms to economic governance, including greater surveillance of national budgets by the European Commission, and an early warning mechanism that would prevent or correct macroeconomic imbalances within and between member states.

Proposals to Increase Funding for the IMF. In December 2011, EU leaders also pledged to extend €200 billion (about $265 billion) in bilateral lines of credit to the IMF, leaving open the possibility that other countries outside of Europe could also contribute to the IMF. News reports in January 2012 indicate that the IMF is considering raising as much as $500 billion in new money to lend, plus $100 billion as a cash buffer, including the €200 billion (about $265 billion) pledged by European countries.[21] U.S. Treasury Secretary Timothy Geithner has indicated that the United States will not contribute additional funds to the IMF as part of this effort.[22] In general, the status of increasing IMF resources is unclear, with the UK government reportedly indicating it would consider sending more money to the IMF only after Europeans demonstrated a stronger commitment to resolving the crisis. The Prime Minister of China has indicated he would consider increasing financial commitments to the IMF in order to support Europe, but analysts question what kind of trade or political concessions China may seek in exchange for this assistance.[23]

Political Dynamics of the Crisis Response: The Role of Germany and France

The leaders of the Eurozone's two largest economies — German Chancellor Angela Merkel and French President Nicolas Sarkozy — have been at the forefront of the EU's crisis response. Merkel and Sarkozy have consistently emphasized their solidarity and have worked closely together to address many aspects of the crisis. However, the crisis has also exposed fundamental disagreements between the two leaders that reflect broader divisions within the Eurozone. This includes divergent views on the role of key EU institutions and on the direction and scope of European integration.

EU leaders continue to disagree on the extent to which Europe's more prosperous member states, like Germany, should provide financial support to lesser performing economies. Merkel, in particular, has faced criticism for failing to demonstrate clearer German support for other Eurozone member states. German officials have emphasized that Germany is, in fact, the largest national contributor to the Eurozone rescue fund. They add, however, that the prospect of guaranteed "bailouts" would create dangerous moral hazard, removing leverage and leaving little incentive for governments of poorly performing economies to enact politically unpopular reforms.

On the institutional level, one key point of contention has been the role of the ECB. German policymakers and ECB executives consistently highlight the importance of upholding the bank's foundational principles: political independence; and a narrow mandate to maintain price stability. French leaders, on the other hand, have long envisioned a more activist ECB that would play the role of a "lender of last resort," akin to the U.S. Federal Reserve. As the crisis has unfolded, French and other officials have at times argued that the ECB should broaden its mandate and provide more financial support to the Eurozone's struggling economies. German and ECB officials, among others, have been reluctant to endorse such a policy shift, arguing, for example, that "central banks should not be called upon to finance states."[24]

Analysts point to the December 2011 fiscal compact as a significant indication that German policy preferences are driving the crisis response.

Germany has emphasized the need for national governments to reduce budget deficits and debt levels, largely through far-reaching fiscal austerity measures. In the German view, economic growth and economic convergence will not come without significant fiscal consolidation and economic reform. Accordingly, Germany and EU institutions have ensured that financial assistance to the Eurozone's struggling economies is contingent on the implementation of rigorous economic reform programs. Berlin has also advocated the adoption of balanced budget amendments in all Eurozone countries.

Although France agreed to the fiscal compact, Paris has in the past strongly resisted similar measures on the grounds that they infringe on national sovereignty. In analyzing France's apparent policy shift, some commentators posit that Sarkozy only supported the compact in the hope that once it is in place, German policymakers would become more willing to support the increased financial assistance that he believes will be necessary to resolve the crisis. Others note that as the French economy has come under growing market pressure, officials in Paris have little choice but to follow Germany's lead.

Some economists have questioned what they consider Germany and others' narrow focus on austerity. They argue, for example, that severe budget cuts further impede economic growth and that policymakers should focus more on restoring economic competitiveness, particularly in the Eurozone periphery.[25] The European response, however, appears to remain firmly oriented toward austerity and the pursuit of balanced budgets. Critics allege that the fiscal compact announced in December 2011 will do little to address growth and competitiveness issues in the short-term.

OUTLOOK FOR THE EUROZONE: WHAT'S NEXT?

In the short-term, the ECB's infusion of capital into the banking system in December 2011 appears to have stabilized markets and, according to some economists, prevented a banking crisis in Europe.[26] The ECB's long-term refinancing operations are also having the intended effect of lowering Italian and Spanish bond yields, reducing pressure on the debt levels of these governments, although they have been less successful at reversing a reduction in lending by Eurozone banks.[27] Some analysts worry that while the ECB's intervention has bought time, it has not addressed the fundamental challenges facing the Eurozone.

Despite these challenges, some economists are ultimately optimistic about the crisis.[28] They note that many crises have threatened the project of European integration over the past 50 years, but that European leaders have overcome these challenges, with Europe emerging stronger and more tightly integrated than before. They believe that in this crisis too, European leaders and institutions, particularly in Germany and the ECB, will ultimately do (or pay) whatever is necessary to keep the Eurozone from collapsing. But, in the meantime, they argue that it is important for these leaders to be tough in negotiations, in order to compel governments under market pressure to take difficult policy measures and to prevent moral hazard and a "bailout" precedent from taking root in Europe.

Other economists view the exit of one or more countries from the Eurozone as a real possibility. Exiting the Eurozone, and issuing new national currencies, could help countries in the Eurozone periphery regain competiveness against the Eurozone core countries, and promote export-led growth. Exiting the Eurozone could potentially involve huge costs, however. Debt is denominated in euros, and leaving the Eurozone in favor of a depreciated national currency could significantly raise the value of a country's debt in terms of national currency. The technical and legal obstacles to exiting the euro are significant, and would likely trigger capital flight.

Additional significant questions that may remain include:

- **What is the ECB's capacity to calm markets?** Markets responded favorably to the ECB's long-term refinancing operations, but some question whether the expansion of the ECB's holdings of periphery government bonds, both through the collateral posted by banks in refinancing operations and the sovereign bonds that the ECB has purchased on secondary markets, weakens the ECB's financial position.[29] How will the ECB weigh concerns about financial stability with its holdings of securities of possibly questionable quality? If the ECB tightens the liquidity support it provides to European banks, such as raising the requirements for the types of collateral it accepts in refinancing operations, how will European financial markets be affected?

- **How can growth be restored in the Eurozone?** Many economists believe that, at the end of the day, economic growth will be the key driver to resolving the crisis. They fear that the focus of the policy response on austerity will come at the expense of growth. To address growth concerns, austerity measures have been paired with structural reforms aimed at improving competitiveness and boosting exports, but the benefits of these structural reforms may pay off only in the long term. Until the benefits of structural reforms set in, how will governments "grow out" of their debts while imposing tough fiscal reforms? What are the risks if "austerity fatigue" sets in and worsens backlash and social turmoil in some countries? If the EU fiscal compact is adopted, will countries have the flexibility they need to respond to economic downturns in the future?
- **Can Greece's debt be put on a sustainable path?** There are fears that if the Greek government is not able to gain sufficient concessions from its bondholders in continuing negotiations, Greece could default on its debt in a disorderly fashion and exit the Eurozone. Two economists at Citi have recently raised their estimate of the likelihood of a Greek exit from the Eurozone to 50% over the next 18 months, from earlier estimates of 25-30%.[30] If there is a disorderly Greek default or a Greek exit from the Eurozone, how can contagion to other Eurozone countries be prevented? Some analysts believe that building a more robust "firewall" or "bazooka," large enough to provide financial resources to adequately defend Italy and Spain from contagion effects, will be necessary.
- **How can trade imbalances within the Eurozone be corrected?** Some economists believe that the crisis, and the build-up of public debt in the periphery, is the result of fundamental, underlying trade imbalances within the Eurozone, but that the policy responses taken have failed to correct these imbalances. In particular, the focus has been on improving the competitiveness of the periphery countries, in order to lower their costs of production and bolster exports. Is there any role for the Eurozone core countries to reduce their trade surpluses, such as by letting wages rise or becoming less reliant on exports for growth?
- **Can European leaders maintain public support for the crisis response?** Although a majority of Eurozone voters appear to continue to view membership in the monetary union favorably, enthusiasm for

the euro could be waning.[31] Several governments in the Eurozone have fallen as a direct or indirect result of crisis response, and public opposition to ongoing austerity measures has become more pronounced in some countries. Both Greece and France are slated to hold national elections in the first half of 2012, in which current economic conditions and the Eurozone crisis response is the primary electoral concern. Some commentators have questioned how committed a new Greek government would be to the austerity measures taken by its predecessor, particularly in the face of at times violent protests. The frontrunner in France's election, Socialist Party candidate François Hollande, has sharply criticized key aspects of the crisis response, including the fiscal compact. Italy, which is currently led by an unelected government of technocrats, must hold national elections by 2013. What effect will the elections in Greece, France, and Italy have on the implementation of previously agreed crisis response measures? How long can European leaders implement response measures that may be opposed by a majority of their publics?

- **What are the implications for European integration?** On one hand, the crisis has prompted EU member states to move ahead with new and unprecedented agreements that serve to tighten economic integration, including the creation of the EFSF and ESM, legislation for more central surveillance of economic governance, and the proposed fiscal compact for greater economic coordination. The ECB has also expanded its role in significant new ways, and some argue that the solution to the crisis lies in moving ahead with a fiscal union that issues bonds for the Eurozone overall ("Eurobonds"), and in which member states relinquish control over their national budgets. On the other hand, the crisis has also increased tensions among EU member states. The initial crisis debates centered on the legality and moral hazard of "bailouts," and many people in the Eurozone core remain opposed to using taxpayer money to rescue what they consider profligate governments. At the same time, while many people in the countries receiving assistance may recognize the necessity of reform, they could also resent the adoption of austerity programs they perceive as imposed on them by Brussels and Berlin. The tensions caused by the crisis have led some observers and officials into discussions on the desirability of expelling poor performers from the Eurozone; of withdrawing from the Eurozone in order to re-gain an independent monetary policy; or of creating a multi-speed EU in which a group of countries would proceed with deeper economic and fiscal integration.

ISSUES FOR CONGRESS

Impact on the U.S. Economy

The Eurozone crisis poses risks to the U.S. economy. The United States and EU have the largest and most deeply integrated bilateral trade and investment relationship in the world. In 2010, the United States and the EU combined accounted for almost 50% of world GDP, and more than 40% of the world's trade in goods and services.[32]

Exposure of the U.S. Financial System

The Eurozone crisis could impact the U.S. economy through a number of different channels. One possible channel is through the financial system and, in particular, the exposure of U.S. financial institutions to the Eurozone. One U.S. financial institution, MF Global Inc., filed for bankruptcy in October 2011 as a result of its exposure to the Eurozone, and developments in the Eurozone impact the U.S. stock market.[33] Modeling and quantifying the impact of a banking crisis in Europe on the U.S. financial system is difficult. When asked about the exposure of U.S. financial institutions to Europe in a Senate Budget hearing, one witness responded, "I think the honest answer is I don't know, and I don't know anyone else who knows."[34]

One source of data on U.S bank exposure is the Bank for International Settlements (BIS), which reports that direct and other potential U.S. bank exposure in September 2011 to Greece, Ireland, Italy, Portugal, and Spain totaled $717 billion, or 7.6% of U.S. direct and other potential exposures overseas.[35] However, these data do not reflect hedges or collateral that U.S. banks may have in place to lower their exposures; do not capture the exposure of non-bank financial institutions (such as money market, pension, or insurance funds); and do not include how the crisis could be transmitted through the financial system, such as to U.S. banks that are exposed to French banks, who are in turn exposed to Greek banks.

According to the *New York Times*, five large U.S. banks, including JPMorgan Chase and Goldman Sachs, have more than $80 billion of exposure to Italy, Spain, Portugal, Ireland, and Greece, but use credit default swaps

(CDS) to offset any potential losses by $30 billion, putting their net exposure at $50 billion.[36] An analysis by the Investment Company Institute, the national association of U.S. investment companies, finds that U.S. money market funds cut their exposure to the Eurozone by almost two-thirds between November 2010 and December 2011, from $32.6 billion to $11.9 billion.[37] A recent analysis by Fitch, a major credit rating agency, argues that large U.S. banks have been reducing direct exposure to stressed markets over the past year and that net exposures are manageable, but warns that U.S. banks could be "greatly affected" if contagion continues to spread to other Eurozone countrise.[38]

During a congressional hearing in October 2011, Secretary Geithner emphasized that direct exposure of U.S. institutions to the Eurozone countries and institutions under the most market pressure is small, but that exposure to Europe, as a whole, could be "a big deal."[39] Secretary Geithner also stressed that the U.S. financial system is better capitalized than in 2009, putting it in a better position to weather potential shocks. At the end of November 2011, the U.S. Federal Reserve (the Fed) announced a new round of bank stress tests for large U.S. banks that would, among other things, gauge losses from a hypothetical shock related to the turmoil in Europe. Banks had until January 2012 to file their results, and news reports suggest that if previous stress tests are any guide, the results may not be publicly released until April 201 2.[40] In January 2012, the Securities and Exchange Commission (SEC) requested that banks provide a fuller and more consistent presentation of their European positions.[41]

U.S.-EU Trade and Investment

Another channel through which the Eurozone could impact the United States is through trade and investment. There has been concern that austerity measures would slow growth in Europe, depressing demand for U.S. exports, and that the crisis would erode confidence in the euro, leading to a depreciation of the euro relative to the U.S. dollar. Depreciation of the euro against the U.S. dollar would make U.S. exports more expensive overseas and European imports cheaper. To date in the Eurozone crisis, however, there has not been a substantial sustained depreciation of the euro relative to the U.S. dollar (see **Figure 6**), and it is not clear that trade has contracted (**Figure 5**), although risks may remain.[42] Longer-term, a break-up of the Eurozone could have substantial implications for U.S.-European cooperation on economic issues.

Likewise, slower growth rates in Europe could cause U.S. investors to look increasingly towards emerging markets for investment opportunities. On the other hand, a weaker euro could make European stocks and assets look cheaper and more attractive, attracting U.S. capital to the Eurozone. It is not clear to date how the crisis will shape long-term U.S.-EU investment flows.

U.S. Government Involvement

Since the early stages of the crisis, the Obama Administration has repeatedly called for a swift and robust response from Eurozone leaders. In October 2011, President Obama stated that the crisis was "a source of grave concern,"[43] and he has spoken with Chancellor Merkel and other European leaders frequently throughout the crisis.[44] In February 2012, following the announcement of the second rescue package for Greece, Obama welcomed the "positive steps" taken by the EU to ease its debt crisis, but stressed there was more work to do.[45] As the lead on international financial issues within the Administration, Treasury Secretary Geithner has also been in frequent contact with his European counterparts, even, unusually, attending a meeting of Eurozone finance ministers in September 2011, during which he urged stronger policy responses. In January 2012, Secretary Geithner reportedly reiterated the importance of creating a "firewall" around the Eurozone as a crucial next step in preventing the crisis from spreading.[46]

European reactions to the U.S. appeals have been mixed; some Europeans have pushed back against perceived U.S. criticism while pointing out the United States' own economic problems. In any case, while the United States wields an influential voice on the issue, it ultimately has limited ability to affect policy decisions made by and among the EU member countries and institutions.

The Federal Reserve

In May 2010, the U.S. Federal Reserve (Fed) announced the re-establishment of temporary reciprocal currency agreements, known as swap lines, with several central banks. These swap lines had been previously used during the global financial crisis and aim to increase dollar liquidity in the global economy. They are designed in a way which minimizes exchange rate and credit risk to the Fed. The swap lines re-established in May 2010 were set to expire in January 2011, but have been extended a number of times due to continuing concerns about the crisis. In November 2011, the Fed also reduced the borrowing rate for the swap lines, in order to further ease strains in financial markets. As of February 15, 2012, $109 billion was outstanding on these swap lines, compared to a high of $583 billion during the global financial crisis in December 2008 (see **Figure 7**).[47] Additionally, as mentioned above, the Fed is currently conducting stress tests related to U.S. bank exposure to turmoil in Europe.[48]

One source of concern about the swap lines is over the impact that dollar swap agreements could have on the rate of U.S. inflation. Through the Federal Reserve, the United States has provided the ECB and other central banks with dollars to maintain stability in short-term money markets that European banks have used to fund much of their ongoing operations. In a swap transaction, dollars are exchanged for a foreign currency, say the euro, at a certain price for a specified period of time. As these swap arrangements are implemented and the foreign currency is exchanged for dollars, the supply of dollars increases, which in theory may boost the rate of inflation. The Federal Reserve has indicated, however, that it has a number of options to sterilize, or to offset, any increase in the money supply in order to suppress any inflationary pressures.

Role of the International Monetary Fund (IMF)

Of the 187 members of the IMF, the United States is the largest financial contributor to the institution, and the United States has a leading role in shaping the IMF's lending programs.[49] IMF programs in Greece, Ireland, and Portugal have been supported by the Obama Administration, but some Members of Congress are concerned about whether these programs are an appropriate use of IMF resources. Concerns have generally focused on the unusual nature of the programs, particularly that the IMF has not generally lent to developed countries in recent decades, and that the programs provide a large amount of financing relative to the size of the economies. There are also concerns about whether the IMF will be repaid in full and on time. Proponents of the IMF programs in the Eurozone point out that the programs are consistent with the IMF 's mandate of maintaining international monetary stability, the IMF has lent to developed countries in the past, if not recently, and that as members of the IMF, Greece, Ireland, and Portugal are entitled to draw on IMF resources. They also argue that the IMF has several safeguards in place to protect IMF resources, including making the disbursement of funds conditional upon economic reforms, and that the IMF has a strong historical record of countries meeting their repayment obligations.

In addition to the support to Greece, Ireland, and Portugal, there are discussions about increasing the IMF resources. Some officials and analysts fear that the IMF's current lending capacity, about $392 billion as of February 2, 2012,[50] would not be sufficient to respond to a crisis in a major European economy, such as Italy or Spain. The process of increasing IMF resources is in the early stages, but Secretary Geithner has indicated that the United States will not contribute funds to this effort. As the biggest shareholder in the institution, the United States may want to consider how to balance, on the one hand, ensuring that the IMF has the resources it needs to ensure stability in the international monetary system with, on the other hand, exercising oversight over the exposure of the IMF to Europe and the concessions that countries are looking for in exchange for providing financial assistance.

The Eurozone Crisis, the IMF, and Legislation in the 111TH and 112TH Congress

Member concerns about IMF resources being used to "bailout" Eurozone governments led to the passage of legislation in the 111th Congress as part of the Dodd-Frank Wall Street Reform and Consumer Protection Act, signed into law in July 2010 (P.L. 111-203). Section 1501 of the law requires U.S. representatives at the IMF to oppose loans to high- and middle-income countries with large public debt levels (greater than 100% of GDP) if it is "not likely" that they will repay the IMF. Prospective IMF loans to low-income countries are exempted from this requirement. If the IMF does approve a loan to a high- or middle-income country despite U.S. opposition, the law requires the Treasury Department to report regularly to Congress about various economic conditions in that country.

In the 112th Congress, continuing concerns about use of IMF resources in the Eurozone debt crisis likely contributed to the introduction of legislation in the House (H.R. 2313) and Senate (S.Amdt. 501; S. 1276). The legislation calls for rescinding the U.S. financial commitments to the IMF approved by Congress in 2009. The Senate voted against the amendment on June 29, 2011. This language was also included in a House draft of the FY2012 State and Foreign Operations Appropriations bill,[51] but the language was not included in the final FY2012 appropriations legislation.[52]

On December 15, 2010, the IMF Board of Governors agreed in principle to a package of reforms, including a doubling of IMF quotas, the IMF's core source of funds, to about $747 billion.[53] To be implemented, the reform package needs to be approved by member countries, including three-fifths of the members having 85% of the total voting power. IMF Managing Director Christine Lagarde has reportedly urged member countries to implement the reform package by October 2012.[54] However, the Obama Administration did not request any funds for meeting the U.S. commitment for the quota increase in the FY2013 budget request.

Implications for Broader U.S.-European Cooperation

The United States looks to Europe for partnership in addressing a wide range of global challenges, and some analysts and U.S. and European officials have expressed concern about the potential effects of the Eurozone crisis on U.S.-European political and security cooperation. Successive U.S. administrations have been proponents of a more united, outward-focused EU, capable of playing a larger role in addressing global challenges. Over the last two decades, some analysts and policymakers have viewed the EU's focus as largely introspective, with EU leaders preoccupied with EU treaty reforms, institutional arrangements, and EU enlargement. The Eurozone crisis appears to have again turned the main focus of the EU inward.

In addition, the crisis raises questions about future constraints on Europe's ability to use economic policies in pursuit of foreign policy objectives. The EU is the world's largest aid donor (counting common funds managed by the European Commission plus bilateral member state contributions), accounting for roughly half of official global humanitarian and development assistance.[55] Some observers question whether the crisis could in the long-term limit Europe's ability to continue providing such levels of foreign assistance or economic incentives aimed at boosting stability and prosperity in developing countries. Some commentators suggest, for example, that the Eurozone crisis has hindered the EU's ability to respond more robustly, both politically and economically, to the recent transformations in the Middle East and North Africa.

The crisis could also exacerbate a long-standing downward trend in European defense spending and cast further doubt on Europe's willingness and capability to be an effective global security actor in the years ahead.

Despite Europe's own internal financial problems and preoccupations, others contend that the European countries and the EU have a proven track record of close cooperation with the United States on a multitude of common international concerns. Despite the ongoing Eurozone crisis, the United States and Europe are working closely together to manage Iran's nuclear ambitions, have significantly strengthened their law enforcement and counterterrorism cooperation over the last decade, have recently concluded a successful NATO mission in Libya, and together continue to promote peace and stability in the Balkans and Afghanistan. As such, those of this view remain more optimistic that the Eurozone crisis will not significantly alter the EU's willingness or commitment to transatlantic cooperation.

SUPPLEMENTAL FIGURES AND CHARTS

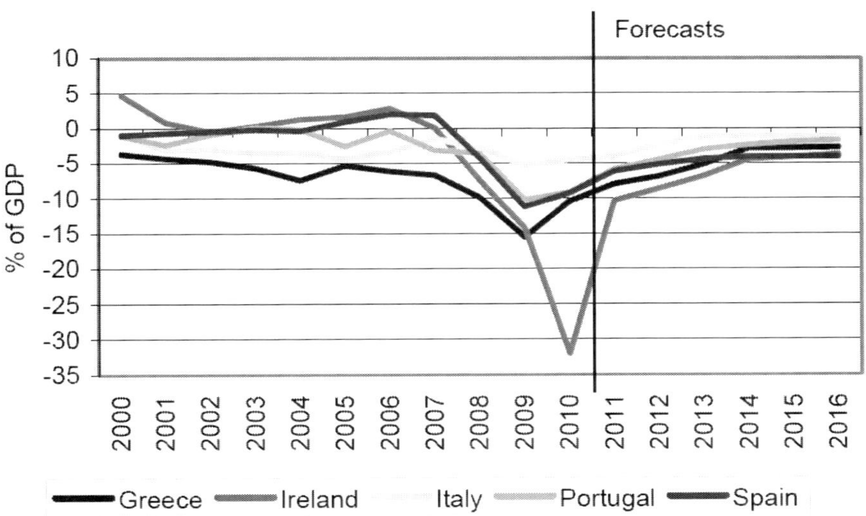

Source: International Monetary Fund, *World Economic Outlook*, September 2011.

Figure 1. Fiscal Balance.

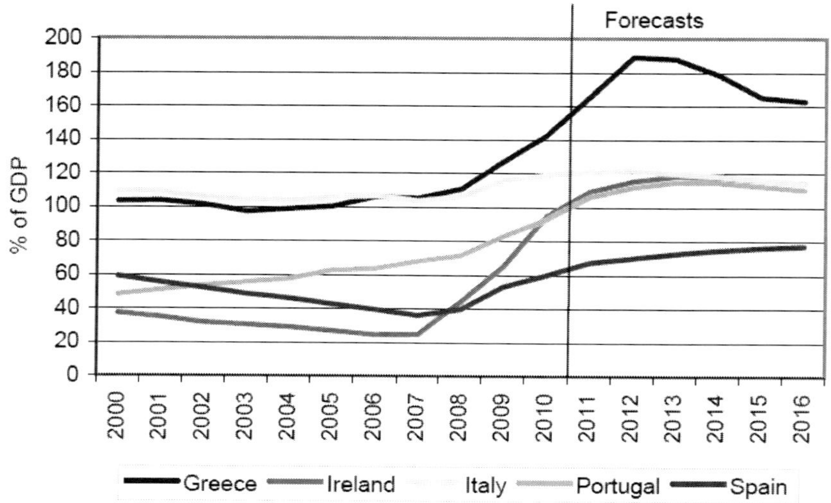

Source: International Monetary Fund, *World Economic Outlook*, September 2011.

Figure 2. Public Debt.

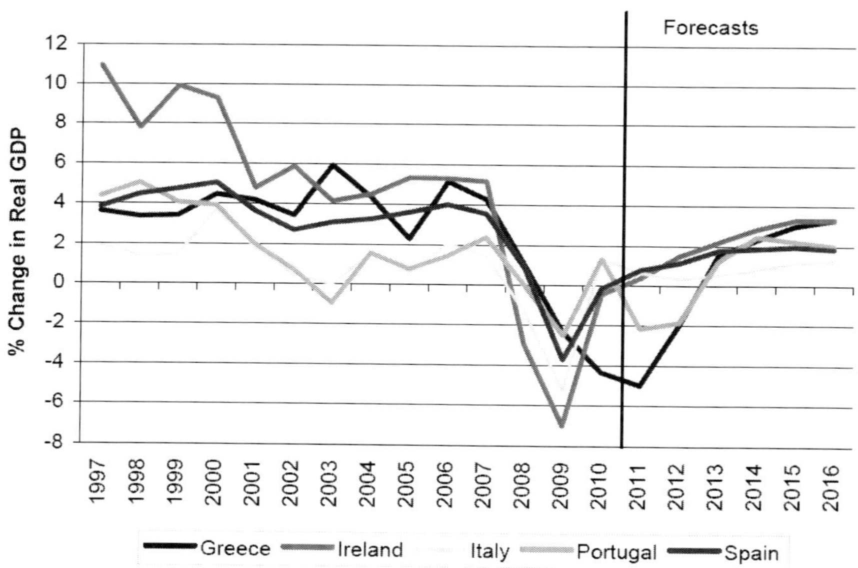

Source: International Monetary Fund, *World Economic Outlook*, September 2011.

Figure 3. Economic Growth.

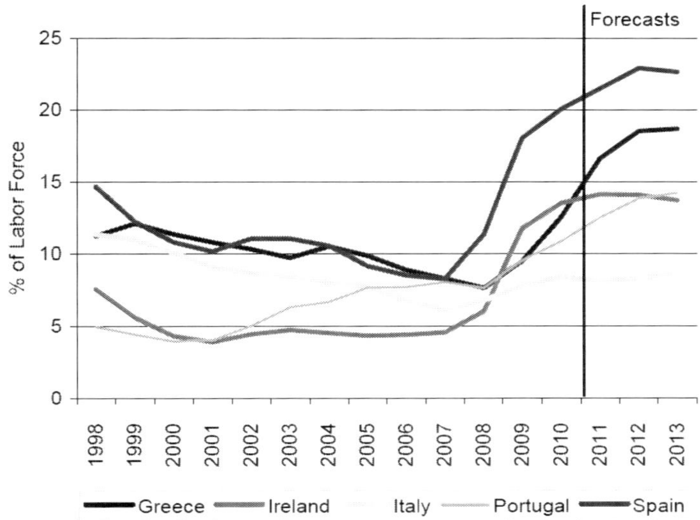

Source: OECD, *Economic Outlook*, November 2011.

Figure 4. Unemployment.

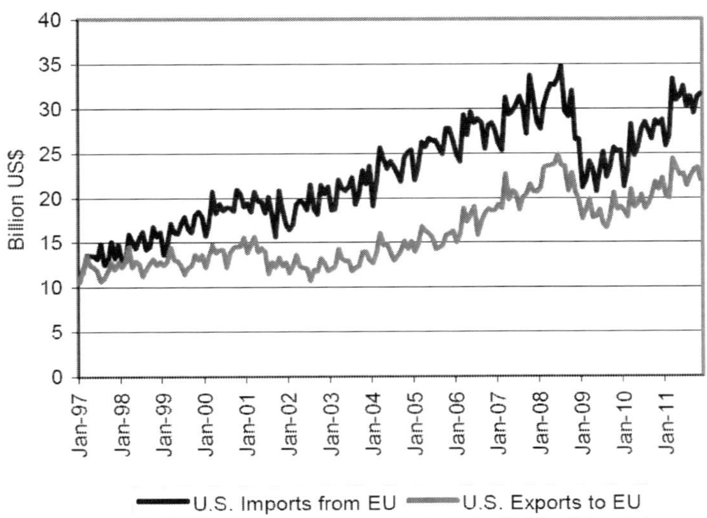

Source: Census Bureau, "Trade in Goods with European Union," http://www.census.gov/foreign¬trade/balance/c0003.html.

Notes: Does not include trade in services.

Figure 5. U.S.-EU Trade in Goods since 1997.

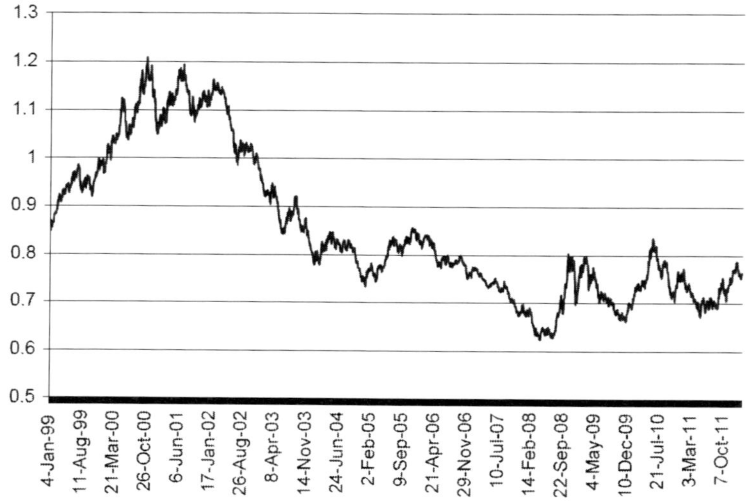

Source: Federal Reserve.

Notes: An increase in the €/$ exchange rate represents a stronger dollar relative to the euro; a decrease in the €/$ exchange rate represents a weaker dollar relative to the euro.

Figure 6. Euro/US$ Exchange Rate since 1999.

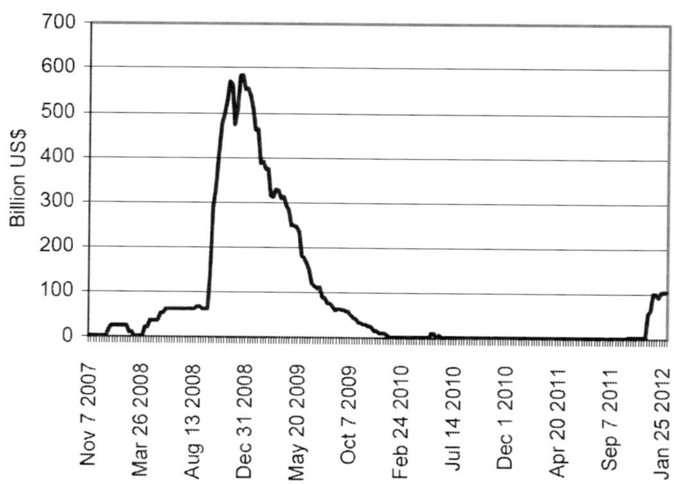

Source: Federal Reserve, http://www.federalreserve.gov/releases/h41/hist/h41 hist13. htm.

Figure 7. Fed Swap Lines, Amount Outstanding.

Table 1. European-IMF Financial Assistance Packages for Eurozone Governments

	Date Agreed	European Financial Assistance	IMF Financial Assistance	Total Financial Assistance
Greece	May 2010	€80 billion (about $106 billion)	€30 billion (about $40 billion)	€110 billion (about $146 billion)
Ireland[a]	December 2010	€45 billion (about $60 billion)	€22.5 billion (about $30 billion)	€67.5 billion (about $90 billion)
Portugal	May 2011	€52 billion (about $69 billion)	€26 billion (about $35 billion)	€78 billion (about $104 billion)
Greece[b]	July 2011 / February 2012	€130 billion (about $173 billion)		€130 billion (about $173 billion)

Source: International Monetary Fund.

Notes: Figures denominated in euros converted to dollars using exchange rate on February 8, 2012: €1 = $1 .3274 (Source: ECB). However, it should be noted that currency swings have been underway during the crisis and the dollar conversions have also fluctuated accordingly. Figures may not add due to rounding.

a. The headline number used by the IMF and in news reports for Ireland's total financial assistance package was €85 billion. This includes €17.5 billion from Ireland's cash reserves and other liquid assets. Resources used by national authorities in the crisis response are not included in the table above.

b. A second rescue package for Greece was originally announced in July 2011, and was to provide €109 billion in official sector financing to Greece. However, the package was pending negotiations, and a revised package of €130 billion was announced in February 2012.

End Notes

[1] A total of 17 states of the 27-member European Union (EU) use the euro as the single currency. The 17 countries are Austria, Belgium, Cyprus, Estonia, Finland, France, Germany, Greece, Ireland, Italy, Luxembourg, Malta, the Netherlands, Portugal, Slovakia, Spain, and Slovenia.

[2] An orderly default typically refers to a government working out a plan to restructure its debt with private creditors before missing or suspending payments, in contrast with a disorderly default, which typically refers to governments missing or suspending payments without previously working out a plan for repaying at least part of the remaining debt with creditors.

[3] German Chancellor Angela Merkel has reportedly stated, "if the Euro fails, Europe fails." Quoted in Howard Schneider and Michael Birnbaum, "Europe reaches bailout deal," *Washington Post*, October 27, 2011.

[4] For example, see "The World Should Heed the IMF's Call," *Financial Times*, January 19, 2012.

[5] Recent hearings include: 1) Senate Banking, Security and International Trade and Finance Subcommittee, September 22, 2011; 2) House Financial Services, International Monetary Policy and Trade Subcommittee, October 25, 2011; 3) Foreign Affairs, Europe and Eurasia Subcommittee, October 27, 2011; 4) Senate Foreign Relations, European Affairs Subcommittee, November 2, 2011; 5) House Oversight, Subcommittee on TARP, Financial Services, and Bailouts of Public and Private Programs, December 15, 2011 (Part 1) and December 16, 2011 (Part 2); 6) Senate Budget, February 1, 2012; and 7) Senate Banking, February 16, 2012.

[6] During the crisis, it has become convention among some policymakers and analysts on both sides of the Atlantic to refer to a group of mostly southern European countries—Greece, Ireland, Italy, Portugal, and Spain—as the Eurozone "periphery," in contrast to a group of mostly northern European countries, including Austria, Belgium, Germany, Finland, France, Luxembourg, and the Netherlands, as the Eurozone "core." In this context, periphery countries refer to the countries that have been under the most market pressure due to some combination of high public debt levels, large public deficits, and persistent trade imbalances, in contrast with the generally stronger economies in the core countries, which tend to have some combination of lower public debt levels, smaller fiscal deficits or surpluses, and trade surpluses. These terms have limitations and mask important differences among countries in the periphery and the core. Additionally, in EU parlance, the terms "periphery" and "core" can be controversial because they may also be used to distinguish between EU member states that support further EU integration and those that do not. Despite such difficulties, this report uses the terms "core" and "periphery" but only to distinguish between these Eurozone countries under considerable market pressures and those in stronger fiscal and economic positions.

[7] In some countries, such as Greece, borrowing was primarily undertaken by the government. In others, such as Spain and Ireland, private sector debt rose.

[8] "Portugal's Problems: The Next Special Case?," *Economist*, February 4, 2012.

[9] Throughout the report, values denominated in euros are converted to U.S. dollars using the exchange rate on February 8, 2012: €1 = $ 1.3274 (Source: ECB). However, the exchange rate has fluctuated over the course of the crisis, and dollar conversions should be used as approximations.

[10] International Monetary Fund, *World Economic Outlook*, September 2011.

[11] For example, see Tyler Cowen, "Euro vs. Invasion of the Zombie Banks," *New York Times*, April 16, 2011; Megan McArdle, "Is the Other Shoe Dropping in Europe?", *The Atlantic*, August 4, 2011.

[12] European Banking Authority, "The EBA Publishes Recommendation and Final Results of Bank Recapitalization Plan as Part of Co-ordinated Measures to Restore Confidence in the Banking Sector," December 8, 2011, http://eba.europa.eu/News--Communications/Year/2011/The-EBA-publishes-Recommendation-and-final-results.aspx.

[13] Huw Jones and Steve Slater, "EU Watchdog to Assess Bank Recapitalization Plans," *Reuters*, February 7, 2012.

[14] International Monetary Fund (IMF), "World Economic Outlook Update: Global Recovery Stalls, Downside Risks Intensify," January 24, 2012, http://www.imf.org/external/pubs/ft/weo/2012/update/01/index.htm#tbl1.

[15] Organization for Economic Cooperation and Development (OECD), *Economic Outlook*, No. 90, November 28, 2011, http://www.oecd.org/oecdEconomicOutlook.

[16] Eurostat data as reported in "Labour Reform in Spain: Spanish Practices," *Economist*, February 18, 2012.

[17] Credit default swaps (CDS) are contracts that provide protection against default by third parties, similar to insurance. For more information, see CRS Report RS22932, *Credit Default Swaps: Frequently Asked Questions*, by Edward V. Murphy and Rena S. Miller; and CRS Report R41932, *Treasury Securities and the U.S. Sovereign Credit Default Swap Market*, by D. Andrew Austin and Rena S. Miller.
[18] "Euro Summit Statement," October 26, 2011, http://www.consilium.europa.eu/uedocs/cms_data/docs/pressdata/en/ec/125644.pdf.
[19] *Economist*, "The Euro Crisis: Checking In on Europe," January 20, 2012.
[20] For example, see Ralph Atkins, "The ECB and its Greek Bonds," *Financial Times*, January 23, 2012.
[21] Annie Lowrey, "I.M.F. Seeks $500 Billion More to Lend as It Plans to Cut Growth Forecast," *New York Times*, January 18, 2012.
[22] Forbes, "Geithner to EU: IMF Will Play a Role, But Without Fed Money," December 6, 2011, http://www.forbes.com/sites/heatherstruck/2011/12/06/geithner-to-eu-imf-will-play-a-role-but-without-u-s-aid/.
[23] Keith Bradsher and Liz Alderman, "China Considers Offering Aid in Europe's Debt Crisis," *New York Times*, February 2, 2012.
[24] German finance minister Wolfgang Schaeuble, as quoted in Marcus Walker and Charles Forelle, "Europe's Options: Few, and Shrinking," *Wall Street Journal*, October 22-23, 2011.
[25] See, for example, Martin Wolf, "First Aid is not a Cure," *Financial Times*, October 11, 2011.
[26] Simone Foxman, "6 Top Economists Answer: Is the Euro Crisis Over? And If Not, What's Next?," *Business Insider*, January 23, 2012.
[27] "The Euro Crisis: The ECB's Tricky Route to Stabilisation," *Economist,* February 2, 2012.
[28] C. Fred Bergsten and Jacob Funk Kirkegaard, "The Coming Resolution of the European Crisis," *Peterson Institute for International Economics*, Policy Brief Number PB12-1, January 2012, http://piie.com/publications/pb/pb12-1.pdf.
[29] For example, see Javier E. David, "Swelling ECB Balance Sheet Brings Relief, Poses Risk for Euro," *Dow Jones*, January 12, 2012.
[30] Willem Buiter and Ebrahim Rahbari, as reported in Kate Mackenzie and Joseph Cotterill, "Grexit," *FT Alphaville*, February 7, 2012.
[31] In a November 2011 public opinion survey, 63% of French respondents, 52% of Spanish respondents, 47% of Italian respondents, and 46% of German respondents said they did not think the euro had been good for their economy. See U.S. Department of State, Office of Opinion Research, *Opinion Analysis: West Europeans on the Euro: Too Big to Fail?*, February 10, 2012.
[32] World Bank, *World Development Indicators*, 2010. For more on U.S.-EU economic relations, see CRS Report RL30608, *EU-U.S. Economic Ties: Framework, Scope, and Magnitude*, by William H. Cooper.
[33] For more on MF Global, Inc. see CRS Report R42091, *The MF Global Bankruptcy and Missing Customer Funds*, by Rena S. Miller.
[34] Simon Johnson, Senate Budget Hearing, February 1, 2012.
[35] Exposure to public and private sectors. "Other potential exposures" includes derivative contracts, guarantees extended, and credit commitments. Bank for International Settlements (BIS), *Consolidated Banking Statistics*, "Table 9E: Foreign Exposures on Selected Individual Countries, Ultimate Risk Basis," October 20, 2011 (Preliminary Report for June 2011), http://www.bis.org/statistics/consstats.htm.
[36] Peter Eavis, "U.S. Banks Tally Their Exposure to Europe's Debt Maelstrom," *New York Times*, January 29, 2012.
[37] Emily Galagher and Chris Plantier, "Data Update: Money Market Funds and the Eurozone Debt Crisis," *Investment Company Institute*, January 13, 2012.
[38] Joseph Scott, Christopher D. Wolfe, Thomas Abruzzo, "U.S. Banks – European Exposure," *Fitch*, November 16, 2011.

[39] Congressional Quarterly, "Senate Banking, Housing, and Urban Affairs Committee Holds Hearing on the Financial Stability Oversight Council Annual Report as well as Votes on a Few Pending Nominations," October 6, 2011, http://www.cq.com/doc/congressional transcripts-3957612.

[40] Anthony Currie, "Fed's Stress-test Revamp Brings Good and Bad News," *Reuters*, November 28, 2011.

[41] Andrew Ackerman and Liz Moyer, "SEC Asks for Debt Disclosure," *Wall Street Journal*, January 10, 2012.

[42] For more on the exchange rate, see CRS Report RL34582, *The Depreciating Dollar: Economic Effects and Policy Response*, by Craig K. Elwell. For more on U.S.-EU trade, see CRS Report R41652, *U.S. -EU Trade and Economic Relations: Key Policy Issues for the 112th Congress*, by Raymond J. Ahearn.

[43] Remarks by President Obama and President Lee of the Republic of Korea in a joint Press Conference, October 13, 2011. Available at http://www.whitehouse.gov.

[44] See Statements on White House home page, http://www.whitehouse.gov and "Obama, Merkel Discuss European Debt Problems," *Reuters*, October 14, 2011.

[45] "Obama Lauds 'Positive Steps' to Tackle Euro Crisis," *EUbusiness*, February 21, 2012.

[46] "Timothy Geithner: Eurozone Needs a 'Firewall' To Prevent Crisis From Spreading," *Huffington Post*, January 11, 2012.

[47] Federal Reserve, http://www.federalreserve.gov/releases/h41/hist/h41hist13.htm.

[48] For more on financial stability in the United States, see CRS Report R42083, *Financial Stability Oversight Council: A Framework to Mitigate Systemic Risk*, by Edward V. Murphy.

[49] For more on the IMF, see CRS Report R420 19, *International Monetary Fund: Background and Issues for Congress*, by Martin A. Weiss.

[50] International Monetary Fund, "IMF Financial Activities – Update February 2, 2012," http://www.imf.org/external/np/tre/activity/2012/020212.htm.

[51] http://appropriations.house.gov/UploadedFiles/FY12-SFOPS-07-25_xml.pdf

[52] P.L. 112-74.

[53] "Factsheet: IMF Quotas," *International Monetary Fund*, September 13, 2011.

[54] Lesley Wroughton, "IMF Urges Members to Boost Funding Under 2010 Plan," *Reuters*, December 22, 2011, .

[55] European Commission DG ECHO, *Operational Strategy 2011*, November 16, 2010, p. 4, http://ec.europa.eu/echo/files/policies/strategy/strategy_2011_en.pdf, and European Commission, EuropeAid, *Annual Report 2010*, p. 5, http://ec.europa.eu/europeaid/multimedia/publications/documents/annual-reports/europeaid_annual_report_201 0_en.pdf.

In: Economic Crisis in the Eurozone ISBN: 978-1-62081-788-9
Editors: E. F. Young and T. D. Murphy

Chapter 2

STATEMENT OF TREASURY SECRETARY TIM GEITHNER. HEARING ON "EUROPE'S SOVEREIGN DEBT CRISIS: CAUSES, CONSEQUENCES FOR THE UNITED STATES AND LESSONS LEARNED"*

Chairman Issa, Ranking Member Cummings, and members of the Committee, thank you for the opportunity to testify today on developments in Europe. Europe is a key strategic and economic partner of the United States, and we have an enormous stake in the success of European efforts to restore financial stability and secure growth. The U.S. recovery is getting stronger, but the strength of our recovery will depend in part on events beyond our shores, as we saw last year when U.S. growth was buffeted by headwinds from Europe.

Since that time, European leaders have taken a series of steps to address the crisis and we are encouraged by the progress to date. We hope Europe will build on that progress with additional actions to calm the financial tensions that have been so damaging to global economic growth and put in place a stronger framework of policies and institutions to make the European Monetary Union viable over the longer term and help the member countries to strengthen economic growth.

* This is an edited, reformatted and augmented version of the testimony given on March 21, 2012 before the House Committee on Oversight and Government Reform.

THE EUROPEAN POLICY RESPONSE

With our encouragement and the support of the IMF, Europe's leaders have put in place a comprehensive strategy to address the crisis. This strategy has the following key elements:

- Economic reforms in the member states to restore fiscal sustainability, restructure the banking systems, and improve competitiveness and growth prospects;
- Institutional reforms, including the "Fiscal Compact," that establish stronger disciplines on the fiscal policies of the member states to limit future deficits and debt as a share of GDP;
- A coordinated strategy to recapitalize the European financial system, with government guarantees of funding; and
- A "firewall" of funds to provide financial support to governments that are undertaking reforms to help assure access to financing on sustainable terms.

These efforts by governments have been reinforced by a substantial amount of support from the European Central Bank.

The European economies at the center of the crisis have made very significant progress.

The causes of the crisis were years in the making and were very different across the continent.

After the establishment of monetary union in 2000, interest rates across the union fell significantly, with rates converging toward Germany's. This was accompanied by a substantial rise in borrowing. In Greece, government spending and borrowing rose dramatically. In Portugal, Spain, and Ireland, private debt expanded. And in all these countries, as well as Italy, the competiveness of the private sector eroded significantly, relative to Germany.

With the exception of Greece, fiscal profligacy was not the primary cause of the crisis.

In Ireland and Spain, the governments actually ran fiscal surpluses, while the private sector borrowed too heavily, inflating a housing bubble. Italy's large public debt is a legacy of a different era. By the early 1 990s, the country embarked on serious fiscal consolidation, maintaining primary surpluses (i.e., the government's total revenues exceeded total expenditures, excluding interest payments on debt) between 1992 and 2008.

As the crisis intensified, however, public deficits expanded everywhere, and fears of cascading defaults by government, the collapse of the financial system, or the unraveling of the euro itself caused a broader financial panic across much of the continent, with the governments of many countries losing the ability to borrow at sustainable interest rates without support.

Over the course of the last eighteen months, the countries in crisis have put in place very tough and far-reaching reforms to address the underlying causes of the crisis.

Greece has reduced its structural budget deficit, which measures the underlying deficit adjusted for the effects of recession on revenues and expenditures, by nearly 12 percentage points of GDP since 2009, according to the IMF. Ireland, Portugal, and Spain have reduced their structural deficits by between 4.5 and 5 percentage points over the same period. In Italy, where the structural deficit expanded by much less, the government has shaved off 11/4 percentage points of GDP. Each of these governments has further plans in place to move closer to a sustainable fiscal position over the medium term.

These fiscal reforms are only part of the solution. The harder challenge is to address the erosion in competitiveness and restore reasonable rates of economic growth, a challenge made more difficult by the fact that in a monetary union, the member states do not have their own monetary policies or currencies that can adjust, and in Europe today, there is no mechanism for fiscal transfers to help cushion economic shocks.

The five countries at the center of the crisis are also putting in place measures to restore competitiveness. The Italian government has begun to implement reforms to improve the business environment, and developed plans to reform the country's labor laws. Spain has introduced reforms to increase the dynamism of its private sector. Greece, Portugal, and Ireland have also introduced a range of competitiveness-enhancing reforms, including plans for privatization, and labor market reforms and pension reductions.

And these countries are also acting to restructure and repair their banking systems. Spain is restructuring its financial sector, reducing the number of savings banks from 45 to 15. In Ireland, bank recapitalization of €70 billion is now complete and the deleveraging of the system – which aims to reduce banks' loan-to-deposit ratios by almost 20 percent over three years – is proceeding as planned.

For these economic reforms to work, policymakers in the Euro Area will have to be careful to calibrate the mix of financial support and the pace of fiscal consolidation. The reforms will take time and they will not work without financial support that enables governments to borrow at affordable rates and keeps the overall rates of interest across the economy at levels that won't kill growth.

Economic growth is likely to be weak for some time. The path of fiscal consolidation should be gradual with a multiyear phase-in of reforms. If every time economic growth disappoints governments are forced to cut spending or raise taxes immediately to make up for the impact of weaker growth on deficits, this would risk a self-reinforcing negative spiral of growth-killing austerity.

These economic reforms have been aided by actions by the ECB, which has lowered interest rates, undertaken purchases of sovereign debt in secondary markets, and provided critical funding and liquidity support for the European banking system. Last December, the ECB introduced the three-year Long-Term Refinancing Operation (LTRO) and broadened eligible collateral. Through its two lending operations in December and February, the LTRO has allotted over €1.0 trillion to hundreds of banks.

In addition, the European Banking Authority (EBA) has conducted a series of stress tests with new disclosure requirements for the banking systems of the entire Euro Area and required banks to raise capital and take other steps to build stronger financial cushions against the economic downturn and to reflect the higher risks of the assets they hold. European banks have raised more capital, but they have also been selling assets and cutting bank lending to help meet the new capital requirements, which is adding to the financial headwinds now slowing growth.

European leaders have worked with private bondholders and the IMF to restructure and reduce Greece's government debt. Fears of a disorderly Greek default played a significant role in fueling the fires of the crisis across Europe over the past two years, and Europe's leaders have, as a result, worked to contain the risk of contagion from Greece and to insulate the rest of Europe from the impact of the solutions necessary in Greece.

This mix of economic reform and financial measures has helped calm financial tensions. The cost of borrowing has fallen sharply for Italy and Spain. Concerns about bank funding problems have eased. But Europe is still only at the initial stages of what will be a long and difficult path of reform.

The most important unfinished piece of the broader financial strategy is to build a stronger European firewall to provide a backstop for the governments undertaking reforms. The existing €440 billion European Financial Stability Facility (EFSF) has made commitments totaling €192 billion. Europe's leaders have decided to establish another fund called the European Stabilization Mechanism (ESM) to succeed the EFSF starting in July 2012. They are in the process of reviewing options for expanding the combined financial capacity of these funds so that they can make clear to financial markets that they have the financial resources available on a scale that is commensurate with future needs in the event the crisis were to intensify.

The European financial crisis has already caused significant damage to economic growth in the United States and around the world, and we have a strong interest in a successful resolution of the crisis.

The Euro Area accounts for about 18 percent of global GDP. It is a major source of financing for many emerging economies. It accounts for about 15 percent of U.S. exports of goods and services, but a larger portion of exports of many or our trading partners. When growth slows in Europe, it affects growth around the world. And when the fears of a broader European crisis have been most acute, as they were in the summer and fall of 2011 and during the spring and summer of 2010, financial markets fell around the world, damaging confidence and slowing the momentum of the global recovery.

Our financial system has relatively little exposure to the five European economies at the heart of the crisis, but we have significant financial and economic ties to Germany and France and the continent as a whole.

We have worked very closely with Europe's leaders over the past two years, and with the members of the IMF, to help support a stronger European response to the crisis.

The Federal Reserve's dollar swap lines with the ECB, the Bank of Canada, the Bank of England, the Bank of Japan, and the Swiss National Bank have played a critical role alongside the ECB's direct efforts. European banks borrowed heavily in dollars before the crisis, and many lost the ability to borrow in dollars as the crisis intensified. The Fed's swaps made it possible for Europe's banks to borrow dollars from their central banks, which has helped avoid a more rapid deleveraging, reducing the impact on financial conditions in many countries where European banks had lent heavily.

The IMF has also played an important role in Europe. The IMF has provided advice on the design of reforms, a framework for public monitoring of progress, and support for programs in Greece, Ireland, and Portugal in partnership with Europe, which has assumed the majority of the burden. These actions have helped limit the damage from the crisis to the United States and to economies around the world.

It is in the interest of the United States that the IMF is able to continue to play a constructive role in Europe. IMF resources cannot substitute for a strong and credible European firewall and response, but they can help supplement the resources Europe mobilized on its own.

The IMF has substantial financial resources available today, and it has the ability, as it has demonstrated in the past, to mobilize temporary resources if that were necessary to help contain the damage from a further intensification of the crisis in Europe. For these reasons, we have no intention to seek additional U.S. resources for the IMF. The IMF has played a critical role in every major post-war financial crisis, while consistently returning to the United States and other IMF members any resources – with interest – that it has temporarily drawn upon.

CONCLUSION

We are encouraged by the progress that our European colleagues have made over the last few months. We hope they are able to build on these efforts in the coming weeks and months to put in place a more durable foundation for financial stability and economic growth. We do not want to see Europe weakened by a protracted crisis. We will continue to work closely with them, and with the IMF, to facilitate further progress.

In: Economic Crisis in the Eurozone ISBN: 978-1-62081-788-9
Editors: E. F. Young and T. D. Murphy

Chapter 3

STATEMENT OF FEDERAL RESERVE CHAIRMAN BEN BERNANKE. HEARING ON "EUROPE'S SOVEREIGN DEBT CRISIS: CAUSES, CONSEQUENCES FOR THE UNITED STATES AND LESSONS LEARNED"*

Thank you, Chairman Issa, Ranking Member Cummings, and other members of the Committee for inviting me to testify about the economic and financial situation in Europe and the actions taken by the Federal Reserve in response.

DEVELOPMENTS IN EUROPE AND THEIR EFFECTS ON THE U.S. ECONOMY

For almost two years, developments in Europe have had an important influence on the tenor of global financial markets and on the global economy more generally. The combination of high debts, large deficits, and poor growth prospects in several countries using the euro has raised concerns about fiscal sustainability and, consequently, led to sharply higher sovereign borrowing costs--initially for Greece, but subsequently for other euro-area countries as well. Pessimism about these countries' fiscal and economic situations, in turn, has undermined confidence in the strength of European financial institutions,

* This is an edited, reformatted and augmented version of the testimony given on March 21, 2012 before the House Committee on Oversight and Government Reform.

increasing the cost and difficulty those institutions have faced in obtaining funding and reducing their willingness to supply credit.

The difficulties in the euro area have affected the U.S. economy. The European Union accounts for roughly one-fifth of U.S. exports of goods and services. Not surprisingly, U.S. exports to Europe over the past two years have underperformed our exports to the rest of the world. In addition, weaker demand from Europe has slowed growth in other economies, which has also lowered foreign demand for our products.

Financial strains in Europe have also shown through to our financial markets. During times when financial conditions in Europe were at their most turbulent, investors around the world retreated from riskier assets. In the United States, these pullbacks decreased stock prices, increased the costs of issuing corporate debt, and reduced consumer and business confidence. In addition, U.S. financial institutions that were thought to have substantial exposures to Europe saw their stock prices fall and their credit spreads widen.

In the past few months, financial stresses in Europe have lessened, which has contributed to an improved tone of financial markets around the world, including in the United States. The improvement reflects, in part, a number of actions taken by European policymakers. First, measures taken by the European Central Bank (ECB), including implementing two longer-term refinancing operations and easing collateral rules and reserve requirements, have allowed European banks to lock in funding for up to three years, thereby alleviating concerns about their near-term prospects. With the benefit of this support, European banks in turn have increased their holdings of sovereign debt, contributing to lower borrowing costs for some countries.

Second, euro-area leaders, the Greek government, and private-sector holders of Greek debt are taking steps to put Greece on a more sustainable fiscal path. Its sovereign debt has been significantly reduced, the Greek authorities are intensifying their efforts to implement fiscal and structural reforms, and the European Union and International Monetary Fund have pledged a considerable amount of new funds as part of a second assistance package. The Greek economy remains in a deep recession, however.

Third and finally, leaders of most of the members of the European Union have approved a new fiscal compact treaty that strengthens fiscal rules and their enforcement. This treaty represents a positive step toward resolving the fundamental tension inherent in having a monetary union without a fiscal union, and thus should help bolster the viability of the euro-area economy in the longer term.

Although progress has been made, more needs to be done. Full resolution of the crisis will require a further strengthening of the European banking system; a significant expansion of financial backstops, or "firewalls," to guard against contagion in sovereign debt markets; and, critically, continued efforts to increase economic growth and competitiveness and to reduce external imbalances in the troubled countries.

ACTIONS TAKEN BY THE FEDERAL RESERVE

The Federal Reserve has followed developments in Europe closely, and we are in frequent contact with key European policymakers. We are particularly focused on protecting U.S. financial institutions, businesses, and consumers from adverse financial and economic developments in Europe.

To help calm dollar funding markets and support the flow of credit to U.S. households and businesses, the Federal Reserve acted in concert with major foreign central banks to enhance the U.S. dollar swap facilities that were originally put in place during the global financial crisis and reestablished in May 2010. Use of the reestablished lines was limited until late last year. However, in late November, the Federal Reserve agreed with the ECB and the central banks of Canada, Japan, Switzerland, and the United Kingdom to extend the swap lines through February 2013 and to reduce their pricing, from a spread of 100 basis points over the overnight index swap rate to 50 basis points.[1]

The lower cost to the ECB and other foreign central banks enabled them, in turn, to reduce the cost of the short-term dollar loans they provide to financial institutions in their jurisdictions. As a result, usage of the swap line increased considerably, peaking at $109 billion in mid-February. The expanded use of the swap lines has helped to ease funding pressures on European and other foreign banks, lower tensions in U.S. money markets (in which foreign banks are major participants), alleviate pressures on foreign banks to reduce their lending in the United States, and boost confidence at a time of considerable strain in international financial markets. In recent weeks, as market conditions have improved, usage of the swap lines has fallen back to about $65 billion.

I would add that the swaps are very safe from the perspective of the Federal Reserve and the U.S. taxpayer. They present no exchange rate or interest rate risk; each drawing has a short maturity and must be approved by the Federal Reserve; they are collateralized by the foreign currencies for which dollars are swapped; and our counterparties are the foreign central banks, not the foreign commercial banks that receive the dollar loans.[2]

In addition to its actions to reduce pressures in global markets for dollar funding, the Federal Reserve has collaborated with other agencies--both bilaterally and through the Financial Stability Oversight Council--to monitor the potential vulnerabilities of U.S. financial institutions and to work to enhance their resilience in the face of possible shocks to the global economy. Notably, U.S. financial institutions have very limited direct net credit exposures to the most vulnerable euro-area countries, and U.S. money market funds also have almost no exposure to those countries.

U.S. financial institutions do have some gross exposure to potential losses arising from sales of credit default swap (CDS) protection referencing European sovereign debt. However, for the large U.S. dealer banks, these sales have been more than offset by purchases of protection, which would imply that in the event of a sovereign default, U.S. financial institutions would be net recipients of CDS payouts. These positions still carry some risk in that some U.S. banks' counterparties might conceivably fail to make good on their obligations, but such risk is mitigated by the fact that the counterparties to large U.S. dealer banks for sovereign CDS trades are dispersed, primarily across large financial institutions. And in the vast majority of cases, these institutions post collateral to each other to help minimize possible losses.

Although U.S. banks have limited exposure to peripheral European countries, their exposures to European banks and to the larger, "core" countries of Europe are more material. Moreover, European holdings represented 35 percent of the assets of prime U.S. money market funds in February, and these funds remain structurally vulnerable despite some constructive steps, such as improved liquidity requirements, taken since the recent financial crisis. U.S. financial firms and money market funds have had time to adjust their exposures and hedge their risks to some degree as the European situation has evolved, but the risks of contagion remain a concern for both these institutions and their supervisors and regulators. In particular, were the situation in Europe to take a severe turn for the worse, the U.S. financial sector likely would have to contend not only with problems stemming from its direct European exposures, but also with an array of broader market movements, including declines in global equity prices, increased credit costs, and reduced availability of funding.

To address these broader risks, we have been working closely with large U.S. financial institutions. Most recently, on March 13, we released results from our Comprehensive Capital Analysis and Review (CCAR)--a supervisory assessment by the Federal Reserve of the capital planning processes and capital adequacy of large, complex bank holding companies.[3] As part of this exercise, bank capital positions were evaluated under a hypothetical stress scenario that involved a deep recession in the United States (with unemployment reaching 13 percent) and a notable decline in activity abroad, combined with sharp decreases in both domestic and global asset prices. This exercise was designed to capture both the direct and indirect exposures and vulnerabilities of U.S. financial institutions to the economic and financial stresses that might arise from a severe crisis in Europe. The results show that a significant majority of the largest U.S. banks would continue to meet supervisory expectations for capital adequacy despite large projected losses in an extremely adverse hypothetical scenario.

CONCLUSION

The recent reduction in financial stresses in Europe is a welcome development for the United States, given the important trade and financial linkages connecting our economies. However, Europe's financial and economic situation remains difficult, and it is critical that the European leaders follow through on their policy commitments to ensure a lasting stabilization. I believe that our European counterparts understand the challenges and risks they face and are committed to take the necessary steps to address those issues.

For our part, the Federal Reserve will continue to monitor the situation closely, work with our financial institutions and foreign counterparts to enhance the resilience of our financial system, and be ready to use our tools to help stabilize U.S. markets should the situation require such action.

Thank you. I would be pleased to respond to your questions.

End Notes

[1] See Board of Governors of the Federal Reserve System (2011), "Coordinated Central Bank Action to Address Pressures in Global Money Markets," press release, November 30, www.federalreserve.gov/newsevents/press/monetary/20111130a.htm. Similar announcements appeared on the websites of the other participating central banks.

[2] For the outstanding amount of dollar funding through the swap lines as it appears each week in the Federal Reserve balance sheet, see www.federalreserve.gov/releases/h41. For other relevant information and materials on the Federal Reserve's website, see www.federalreserve.gov/monetarypolicy/bst_liquidityswaps.htm. For weekly information on the Federal Reserve's swap transactions with other central banks, see www.newyorkfed.org/markets/

fxswap/fxswap.cfm. Finally, for copies of the agreements between the Federal Reserve and other central banks, as well as other information, see www.newyorkfed.org/markets/liquidity_swap.html.

[3] See Board of Governors of the Federal Reserve System (2012), "Federal Reserve Announces Summary Results of Latest Round of Bank Stress Tests," press release, March 13, www.federalreserve.gov/newsevents/press/bcreg/20120313a.htm.

In: Economic Crisis in the Eurozone ISBN: 978-1-62081-788-9
Editors: E. F. Young and T. D. Murphy

Chapter 4

STATEMENT OF C. FRED BERGSTEN DIRECTOR, PETERSON INSTITUTE FOR INTERNATIONAL ECONOMICS[1]. HEARING ON "OUTLOOK FOR THE EUROZONE"*

SUMMARY

Doom and gloom about the euro abounds. An increasing number of commentators and economists have begun to question whether the common currency can survive.

The economic and financial problems in the euro area are clearly serious and plentiful. The area is in the midst of multiple, frequently overlapping, and mutually reinforcing crises. A fiscal crisis is centered on Greece but visible across the southern euro area and Ireland. A competitiveness crisis is manifest in large and persistent current account deficits in the euro area periphery and even larger current account imbalances. A banking crisis was first evident in Ireland but has now spread throughout the area via accelerating concerns over sovereign solvencies.

I believe that these fears are vastly overblown. The European crisis is political, and even largely presentational, which is key to understanding how the crisis has developed and how it will be resolved.

---

* This is an edited, reformatted and augmented version of the testimony given on February 1, 2012 before the Senate Budget Committee.

The lack of confidence in the euro is first and foremost rooted in a crisis of fundamental institutional design. The Economic and Monetary Union (EMU) adopted in the 1990s comprised an extensive (though still incomplete) monetary union, with the euro and the European Central Bank (ECB). But it included virtually no economic union: no fiscal union, no economic governance institutions, and no meaningful coordination of structural economic policies.

It was assumed by the architects that economic union would inexorably follow monetary union. However, there was no pressure to create an economic union during the expansion period prior to the Great Recession. When the crisis hit, the contradiction triggered severe market reactions that continue to this day.

There are only two alternatives. Europe can jettison the monetary union. Or it can adopt a complementary economic union. For all the turmoil, I *believe that Europe is well on its way to completing the original concept of a comprehensive economic and monetary union and that Europe will indeed emerge from the crisis much stronger as a result.*

The key to understanding the evolution of the euro crisis is to observe and analyze what the Europeans do rather than what they say. They have resolved all of the many crises that have threatened the European integration project, throughout its history of more than half a century, in ways that strengthened the institution and moved the project forward. At each key stage of the current crisis, they have in fact done whatever is necessary to avoid collapse. I have complete confidence that, *in the crunch, both Germany and the ECB will pay whatever is necessary to avert disaster.* The politics of each, as described below, assure this result.

The *problem for the markets is that these central players cannot say that this is what they will do.* There are two reasons. First, a commitment to bailouts without limit would represent the ultimate in moral hazard. It would relieve the debtor countries of the pressure necessary to compel them to take tough political decisions and maintain effective adjustment policies. Second, each of the four main classes of creditors—Germany and the other northern European governments, the ECB, private sector lenders, and the International Monetary Fund (as a conduit for non-EU governments like China)—will naturally try to transfer as many of the financial losses on Greek government bonds or European banks as possible onto the other three, limiting their own costs and risks in the process.

Every policymaker in Europe knows that the collapse of the euro would be a political and economic disaster for all and thus totally unacceptable. Fortunately, Europe is an affluent region with ample resources to solve its crisis—it is a matter of mobilizing the political will to pay rather than the economic ability to pay. *Europe's key political actors* in Berlin, Frankfurt, Paris, Rome, Athens, and elsewhere *will thus quite rationally exhaust all alternative options in searching for the best possible deal but at the last minute come to an agreement.*

This is a messy and indeed cacophonous process that is understandably unsettling to markets and inherently produces enormous instability. Miscalculation, and thus disaster, is always possible under such a scenario. But *the process in fact relies on financial market volatility to incentivize solutions that will ultimately resolve the crisis.* Europe's overriding political imperative to preserve the integration project will surely drive its leaders to ultimately secure the euro and restore the economic health of the continent.

THE EUROPEAN INTERGRATION PROJECT

The entire European project was of course driven by the existential geopolitical goal of halting the intra-European carnage that had persisted for at least a millennium and reached its murderous zenith in the first half of the 20th century. The postwar European leadership, driven primarily by Germany and France, chose the policy instrument of economic integration "to make future wars impossible." The project has experienced repeated severe crises over its initial half century but each was overcome, indeed giving way to renewed forward momentum for Europe as a whole. The overriding security imperative drove successive generations of political leaders to subordinate their national sovereign interests to the greater good of maintaining, and in fact extending, the European project.

Germany also *has an overwhelming economic interest in the survival, and indeed strengthening, of the Eurozone.* Its entire economic model is based on export-led growth and world-class international competitiveness. Before the euro, however, its large trade surpluses would often lead to sharp appreciation in the exchange rate of its national currency, the Deutsche Mark, that would to an important degree dampen its competitiveness and thus its growth.

Now, however, Germany enjoys the best of all worlds: the largest trade surplus of any country (even China) and a weak currency, as the euro reflects the much weaker economies of the periphery (and even France) as well as muscular Germany. Every German realizes that this unusual juxtaposition explains much of his country's ability to prosper through the Great Recession, and the current European phase thereof, that has severely retarded growth and job creation in almost every other country in Europe. They thus realize that it is imperative, in purely economic and financial terms of the national interest, to pay any conceivable price to hold the euro together.

The concept of a common currency was always an element in the region's vision of the ultimate goals of the integration project. Concrete thinking about an economic and monetary union in Europe goes back to 1970, when the *Werner Report*[2] laid out a detailed three-stage plan for the establishment of EMU by 1980. Members of the European Community would gradually increase coordination of economic and fiscal policies while reducing exchange-rate fluctuations and finally fixing their currencies irrevocably. The collapse of the Bretton Woods system and the first oil crisis in the early 1 970s, however, caused the *Werner Report* proposals to be set aside for a time.

By the mid-1980s, following the creation of the European Monetary System in 1979 and the initiation of Europe's internal market, European policymakers again took up the idea of an economic and monetary union. The *Delors Report*[3] from 1989 envisioned the achievement of EMU by 1999, moving gradually (in three stages) towards closer economic coordination among the EU members with binding constraints on member states' national budgets and a single currency managed by an independent European Central Bank (ECB).

Optimal Currency Area (OCA) theory[4] prescribes the characteristics required for a geographic area to obtain maximum economic benefits from adopting the same currency. It can offer guidance to economically rational leaders about whether it makes sense for their country to join a common currency. But it was not a carefully considered and detailed economic analysis that ultimately led to the creation of the euro. It was geopolitics and the completely unforeseen shock of German reunification in October 1990 that provided the political impetus for the creation of the Maastricht Treaty,[5] which in 1992 laid the legal foundation and detailed design for today's euro area.

With the historical parity in Europe between (West) Germany and France no longer a political and economic reality, after German reunification, French president Francois Mitterrand and German Chancellor Helmut Kohl intensified the EMU process as a political project to complete the integration of the

French, German, and other European economies in an economic and monetary union that would accomplish full and irrevocable European unity.

This political imperative for launching the euro by 1999 frequently required that politically necessary compromises, rather than theoretically unambiguous rules, make up the institutional framework for the euro. OCA theory, and the earlier Werner and Delors reports discussing the design of EMU, had been explicit about the requirement to complement a European monetary union with a European economic union complete with binding constraints on member states' behavior. Political realities in Europe, however, made this goal unattainable within the time frame dictated by political leaders following German reunification.

The divergence in the economic starting points among the politically prerequisite "founding members" of the euro area made the imposition of firm fiscal criteria for membership in the euro area politically infeasible. The Maastricht Treaty in principle included at least two hard convergence criteria for euro area membership—a 3 percent limit on general government annual deficits and 60 percent limit on general government gross debt limit.[6] However, in reality, these threshold values were anything but fixed as the Maastricht Treaty Article 104c stated that countries could exceed the 3 percent deficit target if "the ratio has declined substantially and continuously and reached a level that comes close to the reference value" or "excess over the reference value is only exceptional and temporary and the ratio remains close to the reference value." Euro area countries could similarly exceed the 60 percent gross debt target provided that "the ratio is sufficiently diminishing and approaching the reference value at a satisfactory pace."

In other words, it was a wholly political decision whether a country could become a member of the euro area or not. Membership was not objectively determined by the fundamental economic strengths and reform record of the country in question. And it was politically inconceivable to launch the euro without Italy, the third largest economy in continental Europe, or Belgium, home of the European capital Brussels. Hence both countries became members despite having gross debt levels of almost twice the Maastricht Treaty reference value of 60 percent in 1997–98.

As a result, Europe's monetary union was launched in 1999 with a set of countries that were far more diverse in their economic fundamentals, and far less economically integrated, than had been envisioned in the earlier Werner and Delors reports or would be dictated by OCA theories. Moreover, shortly after the launch of the euro, European political leaders further undermined the credibility of the rules-based framework for the coordination of national fiscal policies in the euro area. Building on the euro area convergence criteria, the Stability and Growth Pact (SGP) was intended to safeguard sound public finances, prevent individual euro area members from running unsustainable fiscal policies, and thus guard against moral hazard by enforcing budget discipline. However, faced with breaching the 3 percent deficit limit in 2002–04, France and Germany pushed through a watering down of the SGP rules in March 2005[7] that, as in the Maastricht Treaty, introduced sufficient flexibility into the interpretation of SGP that its enforcement became wholly political and with only limited reference to objective economic criteria and data.

In sum, *the euro area by 2005 was, as a result of numerous shortcuts taken to achieve and sustain a political goal, a common currency area consisting of a very dissimilar set of countries without a central fiscal authority, without any credible enforcement of budget discipline, and without any real deepening of economic convergence.*

Initially, however, none of these fundamental design flaws mattered. The financing costs in private financial markets of all euro area members quickly fell towards the traditionally low interest rates of Germany.

It is beyond the scope of this policy brief to interpret the causes of this colossal and sustained mispricing of credit risk in the euro area sovereign debt markets by private investors in the first years after the introduction of the euro. But the financial effects were obvious: Euro area governments and private investors were able to finance themselves at historically low (often significantly negative real) interest rates seemingly irrespective of their economic fundamentals.

Valéry Giscard d'Estaing, when he was finance minister of France, criticized the "exorbitant privilege" enjoyed by the United States as the issuer of the world's reserve currency, enabling it to pay for imports (and foreign investments) in its own currency and making it seemingly oblivious to balance of payment constraints. *With sudden access to "German interest rates," many new euro area members suddenly enjoyed their own supercharged "exorbitant privilege." Large public and private debt overhangs were correspondingly built up in the euro area in the first years of the new currency and in the run-up to the global financial crisis in 2008.*

European policymakers' initial denial and self-congratulations, coupled with financial markets' failure to properly assess the riskiness of different euro area countries and tendency to ignore the common currency's design flaws, thus conspired to ensure that the *euro area, when it was finally struck by its first serious financial crisis in 2008–09, was hit by a double whammy of huge pre-crisis public and private debt overhangs and a faulty institutional design that prevented an expeditious solution that would be credible to those same markets.*

THE POLITICAL BATTLE TO SAVE THE EURO

During its first decade, the euro area institutional framework was that of a "fair weather currency." The area entered the Great Recession woefully under-institutionalized as a common currency flying on just one engine—the ECB—but without the unified fiscal entity that traditionally plays a critical role in combating large financial crises. The euro area leaders have had to build their crisis-fighting capacity and bailout institutions (the European Financial Stability Facility/European Stability Mechanism (EFSF/ESM)) from scratch, and in the midst of crisis, to prevent their immediate financial predicament from getting out of control while simultaneously reforming the flawed foundational institutions of the area. Achieving the dual policy goals of solving a current crisis while trying also to prevent the next one—and using the same policy tools to do both—is rarely easy.

This marks a crucial difference from the United States. Once the Troubled Asset Relief Program (TARP) was finally passed, close collaboration between the multiple existing institutions in the United States (Treasury, Federal Reserve, Federal Deposit Insurance Corporation) ultimately restored market confidence and stabilized the situation in March 2009. In the United States in 2008 – 09, the economic crisis compelled the Fed to immediately apply the so-called Powell Doctrine—overwhelming firepower—to restore shaken market confidence and give the federal government time to formulate a longer-term response in fits and starts through the TARP. This is a fairly well established crisis response function. The central bank comes out with monetary guns blazing and then sits back and prays that the politicians do the right thing. (Congress did of course pass TARP after initially rejecting it but has not yet chosen to institute a sustainable fiscal response for the United States.)

The ECB, as the only euro area institution capable of affecting financial markets in real time, is a uniquely powerful central bank. Its institutional independence is enshrined in the EU treaty and it is not answerable to any individual government. This has enabled it to function as a fully independent political actor, interacting with elected officials during the crisis in a manner inconceivable among its peers. Quite unlike normal central banks, which always have to worry about losing their institutional independence, in this crisis the ECB has been able to issue direct political demands to euro area leaders—as with the reform ultimatum conveyed to Silvio Berlusconi last August—and demand that they take action accordingly.

On the other hand, the ECB has not had the luxury of adopting the straightforward crisis tactics of the Federal Reserve and the US government within a fixed set of national institutions. The ECB cannot perform a "bridge function" until the proper authorities take over because no euro area fiscal entity exists. Moreover, to commit to a major "bridging monetary stimulus," as some have called for, would undermine chances of a permanent political resolution to the euro area's underlying under-institutionalization problem. Were the ECB to cap governments' financing costs at no more than 5 percent, for instance, euro area politicians would probably never make the painful but essential decisions.

Saddled with administering a common currency, and endowed with governing institutions flawed by early political compromises, it is hardly surprising that the ECB's dominant concern as it manages this crisis has been to prevent "political moral hazard" and not let euro area leaders off the hook. Precisely because Silvio Berlusconi would still be prime minister of Italy if the ECB had purchased unlimited amounts of Italian government bonds at an earlier time, the central bank is highly unlikely to provide the necessary assistance to euro area elected leaders to end the crisis—including the Italian successors of Silvio Berlusconi— unless and until they offer and implement a suitable quid pro quo.

It is imperative to understand that it is not the primary purpose of the ECB, as a political actor, to end market anxieties and thus the euro area crisis as soon as possible. It is instead focused on achieving its priority goals of getting government leaders to fundamentally reform the euro area institutions and structurally overhaul many euro area economies. Frankfurt cannot directly compel democratically elected European leaders to comply with its wishes but it can refuse to implement a "crisis bazooka" and thereby permit the euro area crisis to continue to put pressure on them to act. *A famous American politician has said that "no crisis should be wasted" and the ECB is implementing such a strategy resolutely.*

So far the ECB has been reasonably effective in this strategic bargaining with euro area governments. It has also consistently been willing to reverse itself when circumstances demanded. The initial Greek crisis in May 2010 led to the first "grand bargain" between the ECB (which agreed to set up the bond purchasing Securities Market Program) and euro area governments. Their agreement produced strong commitments for structural reforms in Spain and elsewhere. It also produced €440 billion in resources for the newly created EFSF, which proved to be an effective euro area fiscal agent when the problem was Greece, Ireland, and Portugal. Again, *one must watch what they do rather than solely what they say.*

The EFSF is inadequate when the problem becomes Italy and Spain, however. The ECB and euro area governments have therefore for some time been engaged in a new round of strategic bargaining to put together a sufficiently large financial rescue package, secure structural reform of the two big debtors (especially Italy) and, perhaps most importantly, to complete the euro area institutional house. The EU Summit on December 9, 2011 represented the latest round in this game of political poker.

The December 2011 Summit

The real economy in the euro area has gradually deteriorated as regional policymakers dithered in their management of the complex crisis. This rising "economic collateral damage" has increased the pressure to act and led many to speculate that the euro is facing collapse.

This is nonsense. It is abundantly evident that all the key political decision makers in Europe—the ECB, the German government, the French government, Italy, and even Greece— are keenly aware of the catastrophic costs of such an outcome. Greek politicians know that, without the euro and outside the European Union, their country would collapse into a politically vulnerable economic wasteland and/or experience a military coup (the collapse would be far worse than the economic crisis seen since 2009). Angela Merkel knows that, were the euro to collapse, Germany's banks would collapse too under the weight of their losses on loans to the euro-area periphery; the new Deutsche mark would skyrocket, undermining the entire German export economy; and Germany would once again be blamed for destroying Europe. The ECB of course would not want to put itself out of business.

Those political games of chicken are repeatedly being played by all actors to try to extract the best possible deal for themselves. In the end, all will compromise. It is not a coincidence that Greek political leaders, once threatened with expulsion from the euro by Angela Merkel and Nicolas Sarkozy at the G-20 meeting in Cannes, formed the previously elusive national unity government in one week. Italy moved in the same manner within days of its *diktat* from the ECB. *Once Germany and the ECB feel they have gotten the best possible deal, or have run out of alternatives, they will pay whatever it takes to hold the euro together. Neither can afford not to. But neither can say so in advance or, at the other extreme, risk seeing their bluff called.*

Seen through these lenses, the EU Summit on December 9, 2011 developed in an understandable and promising manner. Two issues were central.

First, after 18 months of accelerating economic crisis, EU leaders finally began detailed political discussions about how to reform the flawed euro area institutions. At German (and implicitly ECB) insistence, the talks focused on a new "fiscal compact" aimed at finally producing for the euro area a set of binding budget rules that will constrain member states' policy in the future. Due to the reluctance of the United Kingdom to accept a revision of the existing EU treaty, a new intergovernmental "coalition of the willing" compact may have to be negotiated among a sub-group of the 27 members of the European Union. Substantial legal and institutional uncertainty and "implementation risk" consequently surround these preliminary political decisions and the crucial legal details remain unfinalized. Yet the fact that 26 (or even 23) European heads of state and government declared their political intention to enter into a new fiscal compact, which will severely constrain their future fiscal sovereignty, is testament to the unflinching will to do whatever it takes to save the euro.

Many were disappointed by this narrow agenda and the lack of discussion of a larger centralized EU budget, like in the United States, or the immediate creation of joint eurobonds. However, it must be recalled that, as discussed earlier, Europe does not have the democratic legitimacy to collect taxes for a centralized budget at this point. Similarly, Europe lacks the compelling "endured in a common cause" (i.e., the Revolutionary War) political narrative that enabled Alexander Hamilton to pool together the debts of individual US states into common Treasury bills and bonds. Italy's debts have been run up to benefit Italians and other European taxpayers will surely revolt if suddenly compelled to pay part of them.

The reality in the euro area is that, for the foreseeable future and unlike in the United States, the overwhelming majority of government taxation and spending will continue to reside at the member state level for reasons of political legitimacy. Only a minor part will be pooled at the supra-national level. Restricting this spending via a new fiscal compact is consequently the only pragmatic route for now, leaving other aspects of euro area fiscal integration to the future.

Second, EU leaders tried to thrash out a sufficiently large financial firewall to restore confidence in the solvency of Italy and Spain. This issue was addressed in several ways. For one, euro area leaders reversed their initial intent to insert Private Sector Involvement (PSI) clauses into the new permanent ESM treaty. This should make it clear that private sovereign bond market investors face the same legal environment in the euro area as elsewhere, making the case for "Greece being a unique case" legally and politically more credible. This should ultimately help restore fleeting investor confidence in euro area sovereign bonds. In the grand game of distributing the costs of the euro area bailouts, private investors will not be asked to take haircuts other than in Greece in the hope they will then lend new money to the other debtor countries as the latter undertake the needed adjustments.

THE ROLE OF THE INTERNATIONAL MONETARY FUND

EU leaders further continued their sparring about the ultimate distribution of the costs of extending the euro area financial rescue by pledging €200 billion (€150 billion from the euro area) in new general resources to the International Monetary Fund (IMF). This would come in the form of loans from EU central banks[8] with the political understanding that the resources would be utilized predominantly to stabilize Italy and Spain. This attempt to involve the IMF directly in the rescue of the two larger euro area economies is in many ways reminiscent of the two-thirds/one-third financing split between the euro area and the rest of the world (as shareholders of the IMF[9]) for the existing IMF programs for Greece, Ireland, and Portugal.

However, given the better economic fundamentals in Italy and Spain and the prohibitively high costs of extending to them the type of traditional IMF programs granted to the three smaller euro area economies, a less politically intrusive and less expensive vehicle for IMF involvement may be found. This will still presumably entail special IMF borrowing from surplus and creditor countries around the world. A number have already said they will participate in such an initiative: Brazil, new G-20 chair Mexico, Russia, and a number of noneuro Europeans. China and other large Asian holders of foreign exchange have been more coy. They have also clearly indicated a desire to diversify their huge reserves away from dollars, however, so new claims on the IMF would presumably look quite attractive to them from a purely financial management point of view.

Total IMF borrowing, and the creation of a "firewall" to insure against default by major euro area countries, should and probably will exceed €1 trillion. Taken in combination with the €500 billion in the EFSF/ESM, the €700 billion or more from the ECB from its previous programs (€211 billion in sovereign bond purchases through the Securities Markets Programme (SMP), €489 billion in three-year loans[10]), *and its essentially unlimited liquidity provisions to the euro area banking system, this amount should convince even the most skeptical market participants that the "firewall" is adequate even for Italy and Spain.*

In now turning to the IMF, the euro area leaders acknowledge that their previous "euro area governments only" EFSF bailout vehicle will not be an efficient mechanism through which to provide assistance to Italy and Spain. While this may seem like a political setback, *going through the IMF rather than the (leveraged) EFSF in fact provides the euro area with significant credit enhancement because it makes it much more likely that other IMF member governments, e.g., China and other surplus countries, will choose to contribute.*

In that way the IMF will quite likely serve as a far better leverage mechanism for the euro area's own resources (€150 billion) than had this money instead simply been added to the EFSF itself.[11] Euro area governments will have successfully shifted part of the costs of any future financial rescues onto the rest of the world. The rest of the world will of course extract a suitable price from the euro area for this service in the form of European political concessions in other policy areas. This could, for instance, be a good time to demand that the euro area consolidate its representation on the IMF board to a single seat (from its current eight) and accelerate the transfer of its quota shares to the financially contributing emerging markets.

Moving toward Fiscal Union

Recent ECB policies have similarly tried to shift the bailout cost to other entities. In his December 1, 2011 testimony before the EU Parliament Mario Draghi famously stated "We might be asked whether a new fiscal compact would be enough to stabilize markets and how a credible longer term vision can be helpful in the short term. Our answer is that it is definitely the most important element to start restoring credibility. Other elements might follow, but the sequencing matters."[12] This was immediately taken by markets to mean that, provided EU leaders agree on a new "fiscal compact," the ECB would be willing to step up its sovereign bond market interventions and largely pick up the tab for bailing out Italy and Spain.

Unsurprisingly, euro area bond markets rallied strongly in the expectation of an official sector bailout from the ECB until the next Mario Draghi press conference on December 8, 2011, when he walked back his earlier comments by stating in response to a question that: "The purpose of the SMP is to reactivate the transmission channels of monetary policy. As I said in the statement to the European Parliament, the SMP is neither eternal nor infinite. We must keep this in mind and we do not want to circumvent Article 123 of the treaty, which prohibits the monetary financing of governments... the need to respect the spirit of the treaty should always be present in our minds."[13] Hence the ECB would not be willing to proactively bail out private investors in the Italian and Spanish debt markets. Those markets fell dramatically on the very day of the EU Summit.

The ECB signal thus sent to EU leaders ahead of their summit seemed unambiguous: It is up to the fiscal authorities, not the monetary authorities, to pay to restore market confidence in the Italian and Spanish bond markets. By turning to the IMF at their summit, euro area leaders indicated that they had clearly gotten the message.

The ECB refused to intervene directly and more forcefully in the euro area sovereign bond markets on December 8, 2011. *But the central bank did effectively bail out the entire EU banking system, and with it many of the private sovereign bond creditors, through a series of additional enhanced credit support measures to support bank lending and liquidity in the euro area. These included unlimited liquidity provisions for three* years, compared to a previous maximum of one year, expanded ECB collateral eligibility to include bank loans, and cutting the reserve ratio in half to 1 percent.[14]

These forceful ECB liquidity measures were clearly warranted given the stress in the inter-bank credit markets in the euro area. However, they also provide a potential back door for euro area banks to use some of the funding available from the ECB to purchase additional euro area sovereign bonds and thereby stabilize markets. In this way, assuming that euro area banks can be morally swayed to make such purchases, the ECB would indirectly provide the financing for private banks to support the euro area sovereigns. This would constitute a below-the-radar bailout of governments by the ECB through the private banking system with the political benefits to the central bank that it does not violate the EU treaty ban on monetary financing.

In summary, the December 9, 2011 EU Summit shows how the key actors in the euro area crisis are still positioning themselves to force others to pick up as much of the costs of the euro area crisis as possible. In the meantime, the crisis continues and may superficially appear to be insoluble. There are in fact several possible solutions to stave off a near term meltdown, however, when Italy and Spain begin their large bond rollovers in early 2012:

- Germany can write a check and agree to expand the EFSF/ESM and/or give it a banking license.
- The IMF can write a check using new resources from the euro area and rest of the world to put together a sizable new support program for Italy and/or Spain.
- The ECB can write a check and begin to purchase much larger amounts of the relevant sovereign bonds.

It remains to be seen which solution will ultimately be chosen. It is possible, indeed likely, that the ultimate package will combine parts of each of the above. But it is obvious that *none of these solutions are even remotely as costly for any of the main actors involved, inside or outside the euro area, as a sovereign default in Italy and/or collapse of the euro.* That is why, once the political pre-positioning is over and the alternatives are exhausted, the games of chicken will end and the political decision on how to split the bill for securing the euro's survival will be made.

THE REMAINING AGENDA

Even the most successful financial engineering in the euro area will ultimately fail, however, if the debtor countries, and indeed the region as a whole, are unable to restore at least modest economic growth in the fairly near future. This requires at least three major steps:

- *The borrowing countries must adopt convincing pro-growth structural reforms, especially in their labor markets, as well as budgetary austerity.*
- *The strong economies in the northern core of Europe, especially Germany, must terminate their own fiscal consolidations for a while and adopt new expansionary measures, i.e., they should buy more Italian and Greek goods and services rather than debt instruments.*
- *The ECB must promptly reduce its policy interest rate by at least another 50 basis points and buy sufficient amounts of periphery bonds*

through the SMP to help push their interest rates down to sustainable levels.

There has been much talk about the infeasibility of achieving the needed "internal devaluations." Germany has achieved just such an adjustment over the past two decades, however, probably amounting to about 20 percent of the (overvalued) exchange rate at which it entered the ERM/euro, through a combination of budget tightening and structural changes like the Hartz labor reforms. At the other end of the size spectrum, Latvia achieved an even speedier and more spectacular correction of its huge current account deficit of 25 percent of GDP and, only three years later, is now combining renewed growth with an external surplus. Italy has previously achieved dramatic adjustment, notably to qualify for the euro in the first place. (Greece never did so and its ability to remain within the zone is clearly more problematic.)

The agenda for the euro area, and indeed Europe more broadly, thus ranges well beyond the financial engineering that is clearly the most urgent requirement to overcome the crisis. Both the history of the integration project and the revealed responses at each stage of the current turmoil, however, suggest that both the historical imperatives and economic self- interest of all the key countries, both creditor and debtor, will coalesce successfully. Watch what they do rather than what they say as the drama continues to unfold.

The final major political challenge on the euro area agenda for 2012 goes beyond measures to address the immediate crisis but rather focuses on the longer-term continuation and direction of euro area institutional reform. During 2012, the euro area is likely to adopt a new and considerably more credible set of fiscal rules and budget oversight regulation. This has been a clear demand from both the ECB and Germany. But while the new fiscal compact will undoubtedly help stabilize the euro area in the future, it must be thought of as merely a beginning of the institutional reforms needed in the region. Fiscal consolidation is not everything and the movement toward further and symmetrical deepening of euro area fiscal integration must be maintained. Following the "fiscal rules first" down payment, euro area leaders must consequently take further concrete steps in 2012 on a reasonable timetable toward the introduction of measures such as eurobonds.

It took ten years for the first serious economic and political crisis to arrive after the euro was introduced. The *most challenging part of today's crisis is to use the political opportunity it presents to get the basic economic institutions right and complete the euro's half built house for the long term.* In this process the euro will develop in a different manner from the full economic and monetary union established in the United States. It will require additional substantial treaty and institutional revisions in the future. But as the US Constitution's 27 current amendments clearly show, faulty initial designs need not preclude long-term success. If the history of the integration exercise and its crisis responses to date are any guide, Europe will emerge from its current turmoil not only with the euro intact but with far stronger institutions and economic prospects for the future.

THE IMPLICATIONS FOR THE UNITED STATES AND US POLICY

The United States has a major national interest in successful resolution of the European crisis. Europe is the largest market for US exports and by far the largest locus of US foreign investment. There are extensive financial linkages between US banks, and other financial institutions, and their European counterparts. A breakup of the Eurozone would push Europe into a sharp recession or worse with sufficient spillover to the United States to sharply truncate our (already weak) growth as well. Europe of course remains our major international ally as well and any recrudescence of intra-European conflict, which only the European integration project has been able to check, could be disastrous for US foreign policy and indeed national security.

The Europeans should of course provide the bulk of the resources needed to resolve their crisis. They are doing so already and I have suggested that they will do whatever else is needed.

But there may be domestic political limits on those contributions in Europe, as everywhere else, and the rest of the world may thus need to help. It did so quite usefully in the initial phase of the crisis when the International Monetary Fund provided one third of the external financing required for Greece, Ireland and Portugal. IMF involvement is highly valuable for a second reason that may be even more important than its money (although the two necessarily go hand in hand): its greater ability to devise and enforce the needed disciplines on the borrowing countries, due to its long experience with such programs and far greater ability to adopt a tough stance toward the borrowers.

There is a growing consensus that the IMF should position itself to play a similar role in Italy and Spain, the two large Eurozone borrowers, both became IMF conditionality would then be even more crucial and because their financial needs, which together could total €1 trillion, could be beyond the capability of even Germany and the other strong eurozone countries. Even if the money were never used, moreover, the creation of such a substantial "firewall" could be crucial in convincing markets that defaults by these large economies would be inconceivable and thus restoring confidence in the overall outlook.

The IMF now has about $400 billion of usable reserves. It *is planning to seek loans from its member countries of $500-600 billion to create a "firewall" of the desired magnitude. The United States has a major interest in the success of this project and should support it strongly.*

Many people believe that the United States, as a rich country and the traditional leader of the international monetary system, should also contribute to the exercise itself. This would be inappropriate, however. *The objective is for the IMF to borrow from creditor countries that are running large trade and current account surpluses* (and to channel these funds to debtor countries that are running large deficits and undertaking serious adjustment programs). The main targets should be countries with very large foreign exchange reserves: most notably China but also Japan, Russia, oil exporters in the Middle East, Korea, Brazil, Singapore, Hong Kong and several others in Asia. Several of these countries, such as Brazil and Russia, have already indicated their readiness to contribute.

By contrast, the United States is the world's largest debtor country. We are running annual current account deficits of $500 billion or more. *If we were to lend to the IMF, we would have to borrow even more from China and our own foreign creditors. It would be far better for the Fund to borrow from those countries directly.*

At the same time, it is imperative that the Congress work with the Administration to pass the legislation needed to implement the IMF quota reforms agreed at the G-20 summit in Seoul in November 2011. That agreement included a doubling of the IMF's quotas, and thus its basic resources, though without any increase in total US financing for the Fund because our increased quota would be fully offset by a reduction in our commitment to one of its earlier borrowing agreements. Even more importantly, it redistributes quotas and thus voting rights at the Fund away from the grossly over-represented Europeans to the grossly under-represented emerging markets, which will be an essential part of the "grand bargain" under which they will lend substantial additional resources to the Fund to enable it help Europe on the needed scale. The US quota and voting share would change very little and we will continue to have veto power over any major IMF decisions, which is why our vote is required to implement the reform package and Congressional approval thereof is so important to promote US interests.

The United States can thus provide crucial support for resolving the European economic and financial crisis through the IMF, without spending any additional money, by supporting both the agreed quota reforms and the proposed new borrowings from major surplus countries. I strongly recommend that the Congress support both steps as quickly as possible.

The final, and very important, point is that we should understand that the euro crisis is a wakeup call for the United States as well. In the short run, the travails of the Europeans have led to large capital flows *into* the United States and the dollar that have contributed substantially to our very low interest rates despite our failure to seriously address our own budget problem and the related downgrade by Standard and Poor. Hence Europe has shielded us from much of the adverse effect of our own policy failures.

But we must remember that the financial markets were pricing Greek (and Irish and Portuguese and Spanish and Italian) debt at virtually the same rate as German debt only a few years ago. When reality set in, the crisis exploded very quickly and those countries were forced to adopt drastic fiscal adjustments at the worst possible time – when their own economies, and the neighborhood, were already very weak. *On realistic current projections, the US deficit and debt numbers will look as bad in less than ten years than Greece's did at the onset of its national nightmare.*

Hence we should regard the euro crisis as a wakeup call for ourselves rather than a source of solace that enables us to put off our day of reckoning a bit longer. The current weakness of our economy and the fact that we do have time to adjust means that *we should combine short-term stimulus with decisive actions now, not just words and new procedures, that will correct our budget imbalance and debt buildup over the next three to five years.* A failure to do so would mean that we have learned nothing from the euro crisis and will come to rue our failures to act as much as Greece, Italy and the other periphery debtors in Europe are now doing.

End Notes

[1] The statement draws heavily on C. Fred Bergsten and Jacob F. Kirkegaard, 2012, *The Coming Resolution of the European Crisis*, PIIE Policy Brief 12-1, Washington: Peterson Institute for International Economics. Available at http://piie.com/publications/pb/pb12-1.pdf

[2] Available at http://aei.pitt.edu/1002/1/monetary_werner_final.pd

[3] Available at http://aei.pitt.edu/1007/1/monetary_delors.pdf.

[4] See Mundell, R. A. 1961. A Theory of Optimum Currency Areas. *American Economic Review* 51 no. 4: 657–665.

[5] Available at http://www.eurotreaties.com/maastrichtec.pdf.

[6] The actual numerical reference values to article 104c of the Maastricht Treaty are in a protocol on the Excessive Deficit Procedure to the treaty. Available at http://eurotreaties.com/maatrichtprotocols.pdf. The Maastricht Convergence Criteria for euro area membership eligibility included three other metrics: inflation (within 1.5 percent of the three EU countries with the lowest inflation rate), long-term interest rates (within 2 percent of the three lowest interest rates in the European Union), and exchange-rate fluctuations (participation for two years in the ERM II narrow band of exchange-rate fluctuations).

[7] See EU Council Conclusions March 23, 2005, available at http://www.consilium.europa.eu/uedocs/cms_data/docs/pressdata/en/ec/84335.pdf.

[8] Note that this means that any loans made to the IMF by euro area central banks will expand the consolidated European System of Central Banks' (ESCB) balance sheet, even if the loans are not disbursed by the ECB itself.

[9] The two-thirds/one-third breakdown is not entirely accurate, as the euro area members are sizable shareholders of the IMF themselves and hence in total contribute more than two-thirds of the total financing of these programs.

[10] One might arguably also add the two ECB-covered bond purchase programs (~€62 billion) with unlimited liquidity of less than a three-year duration to these central bank support measures.

[11] Routing euro area central bank loans through the IMF general resources also provides governments a better "legal fig-leaf" against political charges of "monetary financing" (voiced by, for instance, the German Bundesbank) than if such loans had been used to leverage the EFSF directly.

[12] Available at http://www.ecb.int/ press/key/date/201 1/html/sp111201 .en.html.

[13] Available at http://www.ecb.int/ press/pressconf/201 1/html/is1 1 1208.en.html.

[14] Available at http://www.ecb.int/ press/pr/date/201 1/html/pr1 11208_1 .en.html.

In: Economic Crisis in the Eurozone ISBN: 978-1-62081-788-9
Editors: E. F. Young and T. D. Murphy

Chapter 5

STATEMENT OF SIMON JOHNSON. HEARING ON "OUTLOOK FOR THE EUROZONE"*

Submitted by Simon Johnson, Ronald Kurtz Professor of Entrepreneurship, MIT Sloan School of Management; Senior Fellow, Peterson Institute for International Economics; co-founder of http://BaselineScenario.com; member of the CBO's Panel of Economic Advisers; and member of the FDIC's Systemic Resolution Advisory Committee.[1]

SUMMARY

1) Successive plans to restore confidence in the euro area have failed. The market cost of borrowing is at unsustainable levels for euro banks and a significant number of governments.
2) Two major problems loom over the euro area. First, the introduction of sovereign credit risk has made nations and subsequently banks effectively insolvent unless they receive large- scale bailouts. Second, the ensuing credit crunch has exacerbated difficulties in the real economy, causing Europe's periphery to plunge into recession. This has increased the financing needs of troubled nations well into the future.
3) With governments reaching their presumed debt limits, the European Central Bank (ECB) is now treading a dangerous path. It feels compelled to provide adequate "liquidity" to avert systemic financial

* This is an edited, reformatted and augmented version of the testimony given on February 1, 2012 before the Senate Budget Committee.

collapse, yet must presumably limit its activities in order to prevent a loss of confidence in the euro—i.e., a change in market and political sentiment that could lead to a rapid breakup of the euro area.

4) Five measures are needed to enable the euro area to survive: (1) an immediate program to deal with excessive sovereign debt, (2) far more aggressive plans to reduce budget deficits and make peripheral nations "hypercompetitive" in the near future, (3) supportive monetary policy from the ECB, (4) the introduction of mechanisms that credibly achieve long-term fiscal sustainability, and (5) institutional change that reduces the scope for excessive leverage and consequent instability in the financial sector.
5) Europe's leaders have mainly focused on a potential long-term fiscal agreement, and the ECB under Mario Draghi is setting a more relaxed credit policy; however, the other elements are essentially ignored.

This crisis is unique due to its size and the need to coordinate 17 disparate nations. We give four examples of economic, social, and political events that could lead to more sovereign defaults and serious danger of systemic collapse. Each trigger has some risk of occurring in the next weeks, months, or years, and these risks will not disappear quickly.

1. THE EURO AREA'S LAST STAND

For over two years Europe's political leaders have promised to do whatever it takes to save the euro area. Yet problems are growing and solutions still seem far off. The October 27 and December 9, 2011 agreements of European leaders failed to change the dangerous trends in Europe's economies or markets. The implicit risk of default priced in sovereign bond markets reached all-time highs in the last three months. The trend is similar with bank default risk. The crisis is continuing to get deeper, broader, and more dangerous.

A combination of misdiagnosis, lack of political will, and dysfunctional politics across 17 nations have all contributed to the failure so far to stem Europe's growing crisis. I begin with our view on the main problems that are pushing the euro area towards collapse. I then turn to potential solutions (although we are very aware that the complexity of the problems in Europe renders any solution questionable), and finally I outline several factors that could trigger rapid financial collapse in the euro area.

2. Key Systemic Problems in the Euro Area

Within the complex sphere of Europe's crisis, if we had to pick one issue that turns this crisis from a tough economic adjustment into a potentially calamitous collapse, we would argue it is the transformation of Europe's sovereign debt market. We outline this in section 2.1 and then discuss the economic ramifications in sections 2.2 and 2.3.

2.1. European Sovereign Bonds are Now Deeply Subordinated Claims on Recessionary Economies

In July 2011, Peter Boone and I laid out the case that the euro area's immediate problems, in large part, reflect transition from a regime where sovereign debts were perceived to be sacrosanct ("risk-free") to one in which investors perceived that sovereign defaults were possible.[2] Neither investors nor Europe's politicians understood the full ramifications of no bailout clauses in the Maastricht treaty until recently. With the new risk premium needed to compensate for default risk, some European nations will need to radically reduce their debt levels and change its maturity structure.

The treatment of private investors in the upcoming Greek debt restructuring has made it ever clearer that Europe's sovereign bonds bear substantial risk. On July 27, 2011, the EU Council of Ministers finally admitted that a Greek default was needed—although to date they prefer to describe this default as voluntary, referring to it as private sector involvement (PSI).[3] By choosing a default over bailouts, it is as if the politicians have inserted a new clause into all European sovereign bonds:

> *In the event that the issuing sovereign cannot adequately finance itself in markets at reasonable interest rates, and if a sufficient plurality of the EU Council of Ministers/Euro group/ECB/IMF/the Issuer determine it is economically or politically expedient, then this bond may be restructured.*

Soon after this announcement it was apparent Greece could not afford the proposed deal, and more funds would be needed. At the summit on October 27, 2011, Europe's leaders announced that for Greek debt the PSI "haircut" would rise from 21 to 50 percent in order to provide these funds, while the official creditors promised no additional funds specifically for Greece.[4]

Those nonofficial creditors holding Greek bonds learned a new lesson: They are the residual financiers to European issuers when the troika's programs fail.[5] The Greek press reported that the government was prepared to change laws governing its bonds in order to force nonofficial creditors to bear these losses. For nonofficial creditors, a further clause has thus been effectively and implicitly inserted into European sovereign bonds:

> *In the event of default (i) any non-official bond holder is junior to all official creditors and (ii) the issuer reserves the right to change law as needed to negate any rights of the non-official bond holder.*[6]

We should not underestimate the damage these steps have inflicted on Europe's €8.4 trillion sovereign bond markets. For example, the Italian government has issued bonds with a face value of over €1.8 trillion. The groups holding these bonds are banks, pension funds, insurance companies, and Italian households. These investors bought them as safe, low-return instruments that could be used to hedge liabilities and provide for future income needs. It was once hard to imagine these could ever be restructured or default.

Now, however, it is clear they are not safe. They have default risk, and their ultimate value is subject to the political constraint and subjective decisions by a collective of individuals in the Italian government and society, the ECB, the European Union, and the International Monetary Fund (IMF). An investor buying an Italian bond today needs to forecast an immediate, complex process that has been evolving in unpredictable ways. Investors naturally want a high return in order to bear these risks.

Investors must also weigh carefully the costs and benefits to them of official intervention. Each time official creditors provide loans or buy bonds, the nonofficial holders become more subordinated, because official creditors including the IMF, ECB, and now the European Union continue to claim preferential status. Despite large bailout programs in Greece, Portugal, and Ireland, the market yield on their bonds remains well above levels where they are solvent. This is partly due to the subordinated nature of these obligations. De facto, if not de jure, Europe's actions have turned these bonds into junior claims on troubled economies.

Once risk premiums are incorporated in debt, Greece, Ireland, Portugal, and Italy do not appear solvent. For example, with a debt/GDP ratio of 120 percent and a 500-basis-point risk premium, Italy would need to maintain a 6 percent of GDP larger primary surplus to keep its debt stock stable relative to the size of its economy.[7] This is unlikely to be politically sustainable.

2.2. Crisis Spreads into Europe's Core Banks and Incites Capital Flight from the Periphery

On August 27, 2011, Christine Lagarde, the managing director of the IMF, shocked European officialdom with a speech decrying inadequate capital levels in European banks.[8] She referred to analysis by IMF staff showing that, if European banks were stressed for market-implied sovereign default risks, they were €200 billion to €300 billion short of capital. Lagarde's speech was courageous and the logic of her analysis raised deep concerns.[9] This was the first time the IMF admitted that sovereign default risk needed to be taken into account for the largest banks in Europe. Europe's regulatory regime does not require banks to have equity capital funding for sovereign debt—there is no capital requirement, in banking jargon—so banks accumulated these debts over many years under the assumption no additional capital would be needed. They must now revisit those portfolios to take account for capital needs on risky sovereign debt. However, the IMF analysis of the capital needs to offset this risk was odd. Markets price in a small risk of sovereign default, yet a major sovereign default would be a large, discrete event. Regulators need to decide: Sovereigns are safe, in which case banks need little capital protection against sovereign default, or they are not safe. If they are not safe, then banks need to accumulate adequate capital—raising their equity relative to total assets—to survive plausible sovereign defaults. For example, Bank for International Settlements (BIS) data show French banks in June 2011 had claims worth $109 billion (on an ultimate risk basis) on Greece, Ireland, Italy, Portugal, and Spain (GIIPS); if these nations were to default on their sovereign claims, then French banks would surely experience large losses on the entirety of this portfolio while the repercussions for France's own economy would add further domestic losses.[10]

If sovereign default risk is not removed, then banks need nearly full equity funding to cover plausible states of nature where disorderly defaults do happen. The lesson for banks is clear: They need to reduce exposures to troubled nations and batten down the hatches.

In addition, Europe's peripheral banks are suffering large funding losses as capital moves to safer nations – most notably Germany.

2.3. Macroeconomic Programs: Too Timid to Restore Confidence or Growth

While it may already be too late to avoid extensive defaults, we can still consider what needs to be done to reduce the risk of default. To avoid defaults and restructurings, Europe needs to introduce policies that bring market risk premiums on sovereign (and hence bank) debts down. Investors need to feel confident that, with a 2 to 3 percent risk premium, it is worth the risk to hold onto several trillion euros worth of troubled nations' sovereign debts, as well as the much larger non-sovereign debts.

In a nation with a flexible exchange rate, adjustment is usually achieved with budget cuts and a sharp devaluation. Since euro area nations have forgone their right to devalue, they need to regain competitiveness through price and wage cuts, while even more sharply cutting budget spending. In essence, they need to increase volatility of their wages, prices, and budgets if they are prepared to forgo similar changes that could be achieved through the exchange rate.

The available evidence from the outcomes of the troika programs in Portugal, Ireland, and Greece, as well as the recently announced budget plans in Italy and Spain, suggests current policies will fail at this task. These programs all plan for gradual reductions in budget deficits, implying continued buildup of total government debts, while partially substituting private debt for official debt. In Portugal and Ireland the programs rely on external financing until 2013 when it is anticipated the program countries will reenter markets to finance ongoing budget deficits and ever higher debt stocks at modest interest rates. In Italy, optimistic growth assumptions help bring the budget to balance in 2013, but debt stocks remain far too high. Spain announced it would miss its 2011 budget deficit target of 6 percent, raising it to 8 percent. In Greece, budget revenue and GDP growth forecasts are again proving too optimistic.

Any successful program must recognize the fact that appetite for periphery debt amongst investors will not recover to "pre-crisis" levels, because default risk is now a reality that was not foreseen prior to 2009 and because debt stocks are now higher in the periphery. For example, Ireland is currently running a budget deficit measured at 12.5 percent of GNP.[11] The troika program calls for that budget deficit to fall to 10.6 percent of GNP in 2012. Ireland's stock of official debt will reach 145 percent of GNP in 2013, while it also has contingent liabilities to its banking sector that amount to over 100 percent of GNP. An investor looking at these numbers must recognize there is serious risk of default. Since market access is highly unlikely, who will finance Ireland from 2013 onwards?

A successful program must also take steps to quickly improve competitiveness.[12] The only nation that shows moderate improvement in relative unit labor costs is Ireland, but this is largely a statistical artifact driven by the decline of unproductive industry in the weighting.[13] Italian Prime Minister Mario Monti' s program includes no general wage cuts.[14] In Portugal, the government abandoned attempts to engineer unit labor cost reductions through "internal devaluation" after meeting political opposition. In Ireland, the Croke Park accord prevents the government from further reducing public-sector wages.[15] Despite nearly two years of troika programs, Greek unit labor costs have hardly budged.

With sovereign risk premiums rising, and capital flowing out of the periphery from banks while deficits and competiveness improve little, it is not surprising that peripheral economies are in trouble. The Purchasing Managers' Index (PMI) indicates a bleak picture. It is no coincidence that a new major "downturn" started soon after German politicians made clear they were planning to let Greece default. It is also clear that the troika programs are failing to restore growth.

The stark contrast between unemployment in Germany and the periphery reflects the dynamics of the crisis. The strong core is becoming stronger – German unemployment is lower than it was in 2008 – while Greece, Ireland, Portugal, and Spain have high unemployment that continues to rise.[16] Italy's troubles are recent, so with a sharp recession beginning, we anticipate Italian unemployment will soon rise sharply also.

3. Solutions

Europe may continue to veer towards a major financial collapse. European economies are in decline due to capital outflows from fear of sovereign and bank defaults. Recessions and continued budget deficits only raise the risk of default. Macroeconomic adjustment programs are not strong enough and do not reflect the large measures needed given the lack of exchange rate devaluation. As the GIIPS decline, there is serious risk that other indebted and heavily banked nations in the euro area, such as France, Belgium, and Austria, could be pulled into trouble themselves.

3.1. The Big Bazooka

Some analysts are now calling for a massive ECB-led bailout to arrest sovereign risk and stop this dangerous trend. The general hope is that, if the ECB offered to massively finance the periphery, investors would return to buying those sovereign and bank bonds. Lower interest rates would give breathing space for sovereigns to correct budget deficits and banks to build capital.

To see how feasible this is, first consider the sums required. Any bailout would need to unequivocally convince investors that for several years these nations will simply not see serious financial problems. This means the bailout would need to have enough funds to buy up a large portion of the existing stock of "risky sovereign debts" plus finance those nations for, say, five years. The bailout must buy the debt, rather than simply refinance debt rollovers, since otherwise secondary market interest rates would stay high. The secondary market rates will determine the lending capacity of local banks and their creditworthiness.

We have calculated the sums required to purchase 75 percent of the outstanding government debts of the troubled nations (leaving aside debt owed to official lenders), plus finance their deficits over five years. In this base case we assume troika programs are implemented and deficits decline gradually over five years. The total adds to €2.8 trillion, or 29 percent of euro area GDP.

We can then contrast this with alternative assumptions.[17] The most dangerous risk facing the euro area is if a "bazooka" is employed and yet the troika programs fail to restore growth and improve budgets. We assume budget deficits decline only modestly, and we calculate the financing needed to cover deficits until 2020. Our negative outcome implies nearly €5 trillion would be needed just for GIIPS, something the IMF implicitly flagged when they reported recently that Greece alone may need €500 billion (one half trillion) by 2020.[18]

Successful "bazooka" interventions often occur when the extra financing is no longer needed, so that the financing acts as a backstop but is hardly used. For example, when Poland launched its stabilization program in early 1990, the $1 billion stabilization fund was never spent. The US Troubled Asset Relief Program (TARP) was quickly repaid by almost all banks. This is not possible for the euro area. Some euro area nations have too much debt in the new regime with default risk. In the early days of such a program we expect large purchases would be needed. The ECB would have to drive market interest rates down to levels where private creditors would not be well rewarded to hold the debts. As the ECB purchased the debts, private creditors would be further subordinated, and this would add to their desire to sell their bonds.

There are many reasons we believe such ECB "bazooka" programs won't occur and are potentially dangerous to euro area survival. First, while using the ECB balance sheet may make such risks more opaque, any large bailout still poses potential heavy losses for Germany and other healthy members of the euro area. In the event there is default in the GIIPS, Germany would be responsible for 43 percent of the capital needs of the ECB. Hence with a bailout fund of €2.8 trillion, Germany would be assuming €1.2 trillion, or 45 percent of German GDP, in credit risk. The Bundesbank and other national central banks are likely to refuse.

Second, this measure on its own does not resolve competitiveness problems or large budget deficits in the periphery. It would undoubtedly cause the euro to fall but the benefits of euro depreciation are somewhat muted since Germany would remain relatively competitive compared with the periphery. The periphery will still need aggressive fiscal and wage cuts to improve their deficits and competitiveness relative to Germany.

Third, it would place the unelected ECB governors in a political role they were never destined to play and were legally forbidden to play according to the Maastricht treaty. The ECB could quickly become the largest creditor to peripheral nations, and as their financier it would ultimately need to negotiate budget programs, wage cuts, and structural change. It may choose to relinquish those powers to the IMF, but it would be the true power behind all these negotiations.

Finally, the bazooka could well incite an eventual crash of the euro area. If the ECB embarked on a program to backstop troubled nations, observers would quickly recognize that the potential sums needed to maintain stability could be large. Our bad case scenario implies over 341 percent of the ECB monetary base and 46 percent of euro area GDP might be needed.

For markets, what matters are the perceived future bailout costs. Hence, an announcement of a "bazooka" will lead to varying reactions in markets as the perceived bailout needs rise and fall. Investors could become very afraid if peripheral adjustment programs appear to fail or bailout needs spread to more nations. Such concerns could rapidly cause financial- market turmoil and euro area collapse (see section 4).

3.2. A More Comprehensive Solution

If the bazooka is unlikely and probably won't work, while the status quo is failing, what is an alternative? The focus needs to be on returning the relevant sovereigns to solvency. Once the sovereigns are solvent, most commercial banks will have breathing space to rebuild capital through operating profits and retained earnings.

However, there is no easy means to achieve this. In our assessment, the GIIPS will need to restructure their debts by extending maturities and reducing coupons to levels that they can afford. There is some scope for official assistance to offset the total costs of such restructuring by subsidizing debt swaps. However, the Greek example suggests Europe's politicians have little appetite to provide more taxpayer funds for this purpose.

While preemptive restructuring seems attractive, the needed extent and scope is unclear. Carmen Reinhart and Kenneth Rogoff argue that countries with no lenders of last resort typically run into problems when debt levels reach 60 percent of GDP. Even if we assume advanced European economies could manage more debt, it would not be higher than the 90 percent that Reinhart and Rogoff flag as a threshold for developed markets. Such figures imply that greater than 50 percent writedowns of nonofficial debt in Portugal and Ireland may be needed, while Italian debt writedowns might be close to 50 percent.

If the GIIPS followed preemptive restructurings, Europe's core banks, insurance companies, and pensions funds would need substantial recapitalizations, and the costs of this could draw France and other core nations into debt crises of their own. Hence, any plan to preemptively restructure debts would need to be applied carefully across Europe.

The second ingredient is a far more aggressive program to reduce budget deficits and improve competitiveness in the periphery. These nations need to be highly competitive if they are to generate growth soon given the large risks overhanging their economies. This requires large wage cuts, public-sector spending cuts, changes in tax policy to attract investment and business, and stable politics.

If these two steps were implemented, then a bailout program from the ECB would pose lower risks. The debt restructuring and measures to improve competitiveness would mean far less funds were needed. The ECB's role could be to provide confidence that stability would be maintained—a sensible central bank role—rather than to refinance large amounts of debt and deficits.

While these steps would be a major improvement on current programs, they are hardly likely to be implemented. As discussed in section 2, the troubled nations have declined to implement large budget and wage cuts. Political conditions have prevented them. Meanwhile, creditor nations are claiming there will be no more debt restructurings beyond Greece, and at the same time the creditors are refusing to substantially raise bailout funds needed to prevent high interest rates and default. None of this leads to a credible path out of crisis.

4. Playing with Fire: Ways the Euro Area Could Come to an End

Policymakers often have trouble grasping the danger that small tail risks pose to leveraged systems. As we discussed above, a mere 10 percent annual risk of an Italian crisis is already inconsistent with Italian long-term solvency. If Italy has a disorderly crisis, how safe are French banks? And if those banks aren't safe, how safe is France's sovereign debt? Low-probability bad events can very quickly generate a wave of collapse through leveraged systems.

Our concern is that, when compared with financial crises elsewhere, the potential triggers for a euro area collapse are numerous.

4.1. A Unilateral Exit, or the Credible Threat of One

At a midnight press conference on November 2, 2011 in southern France, German Chancellor Angela Merkel and French President Nicolas Sarkozy for the first time entertained the idea that a nation could leave the euro area. Merkel and Sarkozy chose to take a hard line with Greek politicians and their electorate: either complete the existing agreement or leave. The background to this threat was the tough politics in Greece. After 18 months of large budget cuts and some structural reforms, Greece's economy remains in decline. Prime Minister George Papandreou's government was weak, and in a last desperate gesture he attempted to force further reforms through by offering Greek citizens a referendum with an implicit choice of "reform or exit."

An exit from the euro area can be forced in minutes. The Eurosystem only needs to cut off a national central bank from the payments system and prevent that nation from printing new cash euros. Once this is achieved, a bank deposit in Greece would no longer be the same as a deposit in Germany, because one would not be able to get cash for a Greek deposit and one would not be able to transfer it to a non-Greek bank. Of course, the moment people understand such a change could be imminent in their nation, they would run to their banks and attempt to withdraw cash or transfer funds. This is what is now happening in Greece. The country is losing 2.5 percent of GDP monthly in deposits from banks.[19]

There would be enormous, painful ramifications for all of Europe if Greece or another nation made a disorderly exit. Since there is no legal basis for exit, all financial contracts and indebtedness between Greek and non-Greek entities would have uncertain value as the parties could dispute whether these are to be paid in drachmas or euros. Trade between the exiting nation and the rest of the euro area would dry up. The mere fact that a country did exit would have ramifications for the other troubled nations, most likely inciting further capital flight from those nations and producing sharp economic downturns. This in turn would question the viability of Europe's core banks and some of the core sovereigns. The euro itself would probably weaken sharply, and "currency risk" would be added into the euro.

4.2. The Weak Periphery Lashes Out against Germany, while Germany Fights Back

The political dynamics of crisis invariably pit creditors against debtors, potentially leading to flare-ups that cause creditors to give up. In Ireland, against strong popular opposition, the ECB is forcing Irish citizens to take on further debt in order to bail out creditors of bankrupt banks. In Greece, Prime Minister Papandreou was essentially ordered to revoke his planned referendum, while Greece's opposition leader was ordered to write a letter promising he supported Greece's troika program, despite the fact that he clearly did not support it nor did he participate actively in any negotiations to agree to it. French and German politicians are also playing an instrumental role in supporting Italy's new technocratic prime minister, while they eschewed former prime minister Silvio Berlusconi towards the end of his term. Meanwhile in Germany, "bailout fatigue" has set in as electorates and politicians turn against more funds to nations that, they perceive, are failing to reform sufficiently quickly.

While there are many outcomes of such discord, one possibility is that it leads to a messy grab for power. The troubled nations already have the power to take over decision making at the ECB. They may well usurp control in order to provide much larger ECB bailouts. This would raise concerns in financial markets and could lead to rising long-term yields on all eurodenominated debts. Germany would be forced to pay more to finance itself, and German savers would ultimately be paying for the periphery bailouts through inflation and a weak euro. In Germany this would lead to rising calls to leave the euro area.

Once there is a small risk that Germany could leave, market prices for euro-denominated assets would again change sharply. New risk premiums would need to be added to national debts where nations are expected to have weak currencies, while Germany and other strong nations might see their risk premiums fall even further. Such changes would reinforce the recent trends in which the core nations continue to strengthen relative to the periphery, but those changes would also be highly destabilizing for financial markets.

4.3. Economics of Austerity May Fail

The third risk for the euro area is that economic, political, and social realities eventually prove that the system simply cannot work. After all, the euro area is a dream of political leaders that has been imposed on disparate economies. Few nations sought popular support to create the euro. The German leadership avoided a referendum, and in France the Maastricht treaty was passed with a thin majority of 51 percent. Marine Le Pen, who is third in opinion polls for the spring 2012 French presidential election, is calling for France to leave the euro area and reintroduce the franc. Even though most European leaders are highly committed to maintaining this dream, no one can be sure what the costs are in order to keep it.

A plausible negative scenario is that those costs, in the eyes of the electorate, eventually appear too high. The evidence to date suggests Europe's periphery, even in a fairly benign outcome, will be condemned to many years or even a decade of tough austerity, high unemployment, and little hope for future growth. A good comparison is the "lost decade" of the 1 980s in Latin America when nations hardly grew due to the large debt overhangs from unaffordable debts. However, those nations had the benefit of flexible exchange rates, while Europe's periphery faces a more difficult period with uncompetitive economies. Latin America's problems ended only when the creditor nations accepted large writedowns and debt restructuring.

Another comparison would be the heavily indebted United Kingdom during the 1 920s when the government managed policies to restore currency convertibility after the war. Britain suffered with a weak economy for a decade, before ending in the Great Depression, despite a booming global economy throughout the 1920s. However, this too is not a good comparison since Britain had far more flexible wages and prices than Europe's periphery, with nominal wages falling 28 percent during the 1920–21 recession.

4.4. Markets Lose Patience

Our final scenario is the most likely. Faced with the reality of failing adjustment programs, difficult politics, and rising risks that one or more peripheral nations may rebel, or Germany may rescind its support, investors may simply decide that the cumulative risks mean the euro area has a moderate risk of failing.

If investors decide there is a low but significant probability that the euro area might fail, we would encounter another version of Rudi Dornbusch's astute observation: "The crisis takes a much longer time coming than you think, and then it happens much faster than you would have thought." Here's why: The failure of the euro area will be a calamitous financial event. As Dornbusch famously remarked of the Mexican 1994-95 crisis, "It took forever and then it took a night."

If one believes the euro might fail, one should avoid being invested in European financial institutions, and in euro-denominated assets, until the outcome of the new pattern of currencies is clearer. As a result, a large swathe of euro-denominated assets would quickly fall in value. The euro itself would cheapen sharply, but so would the value of European bank debt and European shares, and most sovereigns would see their bonds trade off sharply. This in turn would make it expensive for even the Germans to raise finance in euros. Despite their impeccable credit record, they would be attempting to issue bonds in what is perceived as a flawed currency.

A small risk of the euro "breaking up" would have great importance for the euro swap market. This market is used by Europe's insurance companies, banks, and pension funds to hedge their interest rate risk. A swap contract allows, for example, a pension fund to lock in a long-term interest rate for their investments, in return for promising to pay short-term interest rates to their contract counterparty. It is an important market that underlies the ability of insurance companies, pension funds, and others to make long-term commitments to provide society with annuities, pensions, and savings from insurance policies. The notional value of these swaps is many times euro area GDP.

The euro swap market could quickly collapse if markets begin to question the survival of the euro. Euro swap rates are calculated as the average interest rate paid on euro-denominated interbank loans for 44 of Europe's banks. Approximately half of these banks are in "troubled nations." So the interest rate will reflect both inflation risk and credit risk of the participating banks. If investors decided that the euro may not exist in several years' time, swap interest rates would naturally rise because people would be concerned that banks could fail and that the "euro" interest rate could turn into something else—for example, the average of a basket of new currencies with some, such as the Greek drachma, likely to be highly inflationary.

If euro swap interest rates start to reflect bank credit risk and inflation risk from a euro breakup, then the market would no longer function. A pension fund could no longer use it to lock in an interest rate on German pensions since it would not reflect the new German currency rates. The holders of these contracts would, effectively, have little idea what they would be in a few years' time. Hence, investors would try to unwind their swap contracts, while the turmoil from dislocations in this massive market would cause disruptive and rapid wealth transfers as some holders made gains while others lost. If the euro swap market ran into trouble, Europe's financial system would undoubtedly face risk of rapid systemic collapse.

This example illustrates why a small perceived risk of a euro area breakup could rapidly cause systemic financial collapse. The swap market is only one mechanism through which collapse could ensue.

On November 23, 2011 Germany was unable to sell as many bonds as it wished.[20] The auction failure caused an immediate steepening in the German sovereign bond yield curve. Some German officials argued this failure was due to "volatile markets," but there is a more fundamental concern. Germany's ability to pay low interest rates in euro-denominated assets requires the euro area be a financially stable region. Today, German yields remain very low and are not at worrying levels. However, if these rates were to rise due to fears of currency breakup risk, then the euro area would quickly enter deep crisis as even Germany would have trouble financing itself.

5. Dreams versus Reality

There is no doubt that European political leaders are highly committed to keeping the euro area together, and so far, there is widespread support from business leaders and the population to maintain it. There is also, rightly, great fear that disorderly collapse of the euro area would impose untold costs on the global economy. All these factors suggest the euro area will hold together.

However, many financial collapses started this way. A far more dramatic creation and collapse was the downfall of the ruble zone when the Soviet Union collapsed in 1991. Argentina's attempt to peg its currency to the dollar in the 1990s was initially highly successful but ended when its politicians and society could not make the adjustments needed to hold the structure together. The Baltic nations—Estonia, Latvia, and Lithuania—have managed to maintain their pegs but only after dramatic wage adjustments and recessions.

More relevant, the various exchange rate arrangements that Europe created prior to the euro all failed. With the creation of the euro, Europe's leaders raised the stakes by ensuring the costs of a new round of failures would be far greater than those of the past, but otherwise arguably little has changed to make this attempt more likely to succeed than the previous one. Small probabilities of very negative events can be destabilizing. A lot of things can go wrong at the level of individual countries within the euro area—and one country's debacle can easily spill over to affect default risk and interest rates in the other 16 countries. The euro swap market is based, in part, on interest rates charged by 44 banks in a range of countries; about half of these banks may be considered to be located in troubled or potentially troubled countries. If the euro swap market comes under pressure or ceases to function, this would have major implications for the funding of all European sovereigns—including those that are a relatively good credit risk.

At the least, we expect several more sovereign defaults and multiple further crises to plague Europe in the next several years. There is simply too much debt, and adjustment programs are too slow to prevent it. But this prediction implies that the long-term social costs, including unemployment and recessions rather than growth, attributable to this currency union are serious. Sometimes it is easier to make these adjustments through flexible exchange rates, and we certainly would have seen more rapid recovery if peripheral nations had the leeway to use exchange rates.

When we combine multiple years of stagnation with leveraged financial institutions and nervous financial markets, a rapid shift from low-level crisis to collapse is very plausible. European leaders could take measures to reduce this risk (through further actions on sovereign debt restructurings, more aggressive economic adjustment, and increased bailout funds). However, so far, there is little political will to take these necessary measures. Europe's economy remains, therefore, in a dangerous state.

End Notes

[1] This testimony draws on heavily on joint work with Peter Boone, particularly "*The European Crisis Deepens*," Policy Briefs in International Economics 12-4, January 2012, Peterson Institute for International Economics, and "*Europe on the Brink*," Policy Briefs in International Economics 11-13, July 2011, Peterson Institute for International Economics. For more background, please see also our paper "*Will the Politics of Moral Hazard Sink Us Again*" (Chapter 10, in the LSE volume on *The Future of Finance*, July 2010). I also draw on joint work with James Kwak, including *13 Bankers: The Wall Street Takeover and The Next Financial Meltdown* (Pantheon, 2010) and, on the US fiscal outlook, *White House Burning: The Founding Fathers, The National Debt, And Why It Matters To You* (forthcoming, Pantheon, April 2012). Underlined text indicates links to supplementary material; to see this, please access an electronic version of this document, e.g., at http://BaselineScenario.com, where we also provide daily updates and detailed policy assessments for the global economy. For important disclosures relative to affiliations, activities, and potential conflicts of interest, *please see my bio on BaselineScenario*.

[2] Peter Boone and Simon Johnson, *Europe on the Brink*, Policy Briefs in International Economics 11-13, July 2011, Peterson Institute for International Economics, available at www.piie.com.

[3] For the definition of PSI in the euro area context, see page 18 in *European Financial Stability Facility (EFSF)*, available at www.efsf.europa.eu/attachments/faq_en.pdf.

[4] At the July 21, 2011 summit euro area leaders called for €109 billion of official assistance. On October 26 they committed to €100 billion of official assistance. The IMF did not provide any additional commitment in October.

[5] The troika is the informal name given to the European Union, ECB, and the IMF, which negotiates the terms of external assistance to Greece and other troubled peripheral countries.

[6] To be clear, this "clause" and the preceding clause are just our interpretations – such clauses are nowhere written down, which greatly adds to the prevailing uncertainty.

[7] A 500-basis-point risk premium is consistent with an annual 10 percent risk that something will trigger a decision to restructure and that there would be a 50 percent mark-to-market loss on bonds under such an event.

[8] Christine Lagarde, speech at Kansas City Federal Reserve conference, Jackson Hole, August 27, 2011, available at www.imf.org.

[9] European politicians first dismissed Lagarde's analysis and later the European Banking Authority revised down the needs to €114 billion. They argued that the IMF failed to take into account a potential rally in the price of safe haven bonds, such as France and Germany, which banks hold on their balance sheets. We believe the analysis far underestimates the potential capital needs since it does not take into account the full macroeconomic ramifications of sovereign default.

[10] Bank for International Settlements, Table 9D: Consolidated foreign claims of reporting banks— Ultimate risk basis, *BIS Quarterly Review*, December 2011, available at www.bis.org/publ/qtrpdf/r_qa1112_anx9d_u.pdf.

[11] Ireland's GNP is substantially smaller than its GDP. Due to its role as a tax haven, many foreign companies have set up operations in Ireland, with a controlling shell company

located in a tax-free nation, in order to take advantage of Ireland's regulations that specify that the controlling owner, rather than the resident company, is subject to tax. For this reason companies such as Google, Yahoo, Microsoft, Forest Labs, and many others channel license revenues and royalties through Irish subsidiaries. These royalties and revenues are in large part excluded from the tax base in Ireland. These companies would move if Ireland changed rules and made such revenues taxable. Since the relevant concept for fiscal sustainability is the taxable base, it makes sense that this should be used to measure Ireland's indicators. No other nation in Europe has a large difference between GNP and GDP. The IMF regularly reported Irish GNP in its staff reports but abruptly removed all reference to GNP in the most recent report. This raises concerns that the IMF is attempting to mask fiscal sustainability problems by not reporting these data.

[12] Unit labor costs are the best measure of competitiveness in this context. These also include nontraded goods and are not a perfect measure of competitiveness, but the general pattern is clear – over the past decade Germany has really diverged from its European trading partners by becoming more competitive.

[13] Ireland's nontraded goods sector is less productive than its traded goods sector (which includes companies such as Google that choose to report earnings in this low corporate tax environment.) As part of the Irish recession, the nontraded goods sector has contracted while "exports" from large multinationals have remained relatively robust.

[14] See, for example, Alex Roe, "Monti's Measures for Italy," *Italy Chronicles*, December 5, 2011, available at http://italychronicles.com.

[15] See Harry McGee, "Freeze on cuts after Croke Park accord," *Irish Times*, July 21, 2011, available at www.irishtimes.com.

[16] The latest unemployment numbers are bad, including 22 percent in Spain and 14 percent in Ireland.

[17] For more detail, please see Peter Boone and Simon Johnson, "The European Crisis Deepens", referenced in footnote 1 above.

[18] This is a stress scenario in the IMF's debt sustainability analysis for Greece. In our view, this scenario could reasonably be regarded as something closer to a baseline forecast.

[19] Deposits have declined by €61 billion, or 24 percent of GDP, since spring 2009. See Bank of Greece, "Aggregated balance sheets of monetary financial institutions (MFIs)," available at www.bankofgreece.gr.

[20] Paul Dobson, "German Auction 'Disaster' Stirs Crisis Concern," Bloomberg News, November 23, 2011, available at www.bloomberg.com.

In: Economic Crisis in the Eurozone ISBN: 978-1-62081-788-9
Editors: E. F. Young and T. D. Murphy

Chapter 6

STATEMENT OF ADAM LERRICK, SCHOLAR FROM THE AMERICAN ENTERPRISE INSTITUTE. HEARING ON "OUTLOOK FOR THE EUROZONE"*

It is a privilege to appear before the Senate Committee on the Budget.

Europe's crisis is not a currency crisis. Sound monetary policy has kept the Euro at $1.30 within its past range of $0.85-1.60. Europe has a fiscal crisis compounded by a failure to take corrective action that has destroyed its credibility in the capital markets.

I. SELF-INFLICTED CRISIS: NO DISCIPLINE AND CREDULOUS MARKETS

The European monetary union limited government deficits to 3% of GDP and national debt to 60% of GDP. Markets accepted this fiscal performance guarantee at face value and believed sovereign credit risk was homogenized. The interest rate differential between the strongest member Germany and the weakest member Greece fell from 8% per annum to 0.2%.

However, the fiscal rules were never enforced. By 2006, 7 of the original 12 members were over the 60% debt limit. By 2010, 10 exceeded the limit. Weak governments used massive borrowing to offer their citizens a standard of living their productivity could not deliver. The crisis began in October 2009

* This is an edited, reformatted and augmented version of the testimony given on 1 February 2012 before the Senate Budget Committee.

when Greece announced a doubling of its fiscal deficit and markets saw their error. Two years ago, Greece should have defaulted on its debt and other spendthrift governments should have tightened their budgets.

The fundamental problem is that European policymakers do not understand markets, do not like markets and believe they can control markets. They live in financial pre-history and always choose pressure and regulation over incentives and market forces.

II. Disagreement over the Responsibility of Members: Accountability versus Solidarity

Europe's inability to act in the face of a crisis stems from a core disagreement over the responsibilities of Union members. Without fundamental agreement, all actions have been failed political compromises that further erode market credibility.

Germany leads the North. The cause of the crisis is a lack of discipline in the South. Profligate members must cut spending, lower wages and increase productivity. The path Germany itself used to gain its current prosperity. Each member is responsible for its own fiscal and economic wellbeing. If markets see credible action, interest rates will fall and the crisis will end.

Southern Europe believes their troubles are caused by Germany's success. Union solidarity requires massive transfers from strong members to the weak. A collectivized Eurobond will lower financing costs and minimize adjustment pain.

France, instead of siding with other AAA members, has appointed itself head of the South to capture European political leadership while leaving the cost of bailouts with Germany.

III. The Monetary Printing Press: Mimicking the Federal Reserve

Germany wants immediate strong fiscal correction by individual governments. The rest of Europe and the Obama administration want a quick fix where the European Central Bank (ECB) prints EUR 2 trillion and buys every weak government bond in sight until yields are driven down to 4%. They believe the real problem can be dealt with later.

Germany disagrees. If a long term solution is not offered, no amount of money will make stop-gap measures work. If Germany capitulates, a currency crisis will be added to Europe's fiscal crisis.

IV. Stable Monetary Union and Collectivized Euro-bonds

Since the Euro's inception, members have struggled with the conflict between central control and national sovereignty.

There are two forms of stable monetary union:

1. Members share a currency but each government stands on its own before its creditors. Markets take losses, impose discipline and set borrowing limits; or
2. The Union underwrites all its members. Then the Union takes losses and must impose discipline and set member debt and spending limits.

A monetary union that cannot make up its mind is a crisis waiting to happen and Europe is still struggling to make up its mind.

The debate over the creation of common liability Euro-bonds is a false argument. If fiscal control is achieved: There is no need. All members will be AAA. Without control: Eurobonds are not viable. As one of the German Parliament's Economic Policy leaders said: "They are the devil's work".

V. Germany's Vision: The Next Level of Europe

Germany has now found the tools to force Union fiscal discipline after two years of reasoning, threatening and pleading had no effect.

Market forces can succeed where diplomacy fails. Painfully high interest rates compel politicians to make necessary choices. Removal of the unanimity requirement on Euro-zone decisions takes away the veto right of prodigal members. There will be no access to emergency aid without agreement to the fiscal compact. The fear of being left behind without support will force submission to fiscal reform.

Over the next 2-3 years, Germany will drive the Euro-zone toward a fiscal union with central control over national budgets and strong automatic sanctions against spending offenders.

This is a difficult path. The greatest danger is that if a crisis looms, politicians will confuse the end of their world with the end of the world, bail out every government and bank in sight and set economic stability back a decade.

The strong arm of the ECB is needed to support the path to the European fiscal compact and maintain stability in fragile markets. The ECB should announce a rule of intervention that removes the risk of financial panic but preserves incentives for investors and politicians and safe-guards its inflation-fighting credibility.

VI. Europe's Long Term Problem

Europe's excess debt can be solved: write it down. Europe's excess deficits can be solved: cut spending.

The difficult problem is that Southern Europe's populations expect a life-style their productivity cannot supply. Greeks don't have to be Germans but then they cannot expect to be paid like Germans.

The 25% gap between Southern Europe and German labor costs can only be closed by nominal deflation because devaluation is not possible within the currency union. This is a long painful process that will precipitate a 5-7 year recession in the uncompetitive economies.

The only other alternative is a long term transfer from Europe's productive North to the easygoing South. The reunification of Germany posed the same problem of differing productivity. A solidarity tax was imposed to bring the former East Germany up to West German standards. Envisaged as a temporary transition mechanism, it is still in full force 20 years later.

Northern Europe will pay the transfer directly through taxes and aid and indirectly through higher inflation to reduce Southern Europe's debt.

In: Economic Crisis in the Eurozone ISBN: 978-1-62081-788-9
Editors: E. F. Young and T. D. Murphy

Chapter 7

TESTIMONY OF LAEL BRAINARD, UNDER SECRETARY FOR INTERNATIONAL AFFAIRS. HEARING ON "EXAMINING THE EUROPEAN DEBT CRISIS AND ITS IMPLICATIONS"*

Chairman Johnson, Ranking Member Shelby, and distinguished members of the committee, thank you for the opportunity to discuss recent developments in Europe and how we are engaging with our partners to limit risks to the U.S. economy.

EUROPE IS A KEY PARTNER

The United States has an enormous stake in the continued strength and stability of Europe. The Transatlantic partnership is an enduring source of economic and political stability and is a cornerstone of our international engagement and alliances.

We are reminded daily of our unique partnership with Europe. The United States and EU are cooperating closely to increase pressure on Iran due to its noncompliance with international nuclear obligations. We welcomed Europe's decision to ban imports of Iranian oil and petroleum products, freeze the assets of the Iranian central bank, and take additional action against Iran's energy, financial, and transport sectors.

---

* This is an edited, reformatted and augmented version of the testimony given on February 16, 2012 before the Senate Banking Committee.

In Afghanistan, the United States, the EU, and other European donors provide the majority of funding for stabilization, promotion of democratic governance, and transition to a sustainable economy.

I am just back from leading a meeting in Abu Dhabi working closely with our European partners along with our partners in the Gulf and G8 to support the Arab countries in transition as they work to deliver inclusive growth and opportunities for their young people.

U.S. Economic Stake

Our economic stake in Europe is also immense. The United States has no bigger, no more important economic relationship than it does with Europe. A strong European economy—the second largest in the world-- is essential to a strong global economy and a robust U.S. recovery. Our recovery has strengthened recently but remains vulnerable to events in Europe.

The euro area is currently confronting difficult challenges of fiscal sustainability, of liquidity, and of structural imbalances. We believe Europe has the will and the capacity to manage these challenges effectively.

Nonetheless, if the euro area were to experience a deterioration of financial conditions, this could pose important risks to our recovery.

A further drop in growth within the euro area would reduce demand for US products and services at a time when external demand is an important engine of our recovery. The euro area accounts for nearly 15 percent of U.S. goods and services exports. It is the most significant foreign source of investment and jobs in America, accounting for fully 40 percent of all FDI in the United States. By way of illustration, fully one third of South Carolina's exports and over one quarter of Alabama's exports are destined for Europe, with a particular emphasis on autos and auto exports. Exports to Europe represent 18 to 24 percent of merchandise exports from New York, North Carolina, and Illinois, accounting for hundreds of thousands of jobs that could be put at risk by a decline in European demand.

As Chairman Bernanke noted in testimony, U.S. banks have made progress in protecting themselves against problems in European sovereign or bank debt. Our banks have built thicker capital cushions and better liquidity buffers since the crisis. In fact, the direct exposures of the U.S. financial system to the most vulnerable euro area program countries are quite modest. However, our banking system still has material exposure to the core of Europe and to the broader banking system, which could be impacted if financial stress were to broaden in Europe.

Although we are in a better position to withstand financial stress and contagion, further deterioration in Europe could have a material adverse impact on our financial system. The globally connected nature of financial markets means that stress in European financial markets will be felt in the United States. Volatility in financial markets reduces risk appetite, undermines business and consumer confidence, and jeopardizes the availability of credit. That, in turn, can hurt American businesses and jobs, particularly in smaller firms that depend on credit from their banks to grow and innovate. It could also reduce the savings and wealth of American families.

THE EUROPEAN POLICY RESPONSE

The leaders of the euro area face complicated challenges that will require sustained political will to address over time. Market participants have demonstrated concerns about a combination of slow growth, low competitiveness, and large debts in some countries, as well as a large and highly interconnected banking system. These in turn are symptoms of underlying gaps in the European Monetary Union's institutional framework.

Over the course of the decade since the advent of the euro, substantial and persistent internal imbalances emerged within the euro area, with large balance of payments deficits in Spain, Portugal, Ireland, and Greece offsetting large surpluses in countries like Germany and the Netherlands. These reflected differences in competitiveness, as well as differences in fiscal policy. The internal imbalances were initially sustained by private capital flows, as private savers in the surplus countries financed deficits elsewhere in the euro area. However, in the past 2 years, private financing has retreated. Resolving these internal imbalances is a difficult feat within the confines of a monetary union where currency adjustment is not an option and fiscal integration has lagged far behind.

The leaders of the euro area have pledged to do whatever it takes to stand behind the euro. And we have confidence the euro area has the capacity and the resources to stand behind that commitment. It is a common feature of financial crises that the pace of markets far outstrips that of political process. The challenge of delivering on European leaders' commitment has been magnified by the considerable time that is required to secure agreement among

17 heads of state and permit deliberation and approval by 17 national parliaments. Despite these challenges, Europe has made enormous strides.

For our part, in addition to the actions we have taken domestically to strengthen the US economy, we have been working strenuously to protect against elevated financial stress in Europe. Since the risks associated with Greece first became apparent in early 2010, the President and Secretary Geithner have worked tirelessly with their European partners, the IMF, and their G20 partners to underscore the gravity of the situation and the critical need to act quickly and with decisive force to restore confidence and combat contagion.

The United States and our international partners stand with European leaders as they work to restore confidence in the foundation of the eurozone. We have consistently supported a comprehensive plan to decisively address the crisis with 4 key elements: reforms to address the root causes of the crisis; ensuring European banks have the liquidity and the capital cushions they need to maintain the full confidence of depositors and creditors; a powerful firewall to stem contagion and ensure sovereigns have access to affordable financing as they reform; and charting a sustainable path forward for Greece. Our European partners are making progress on these key elements.

The first priority is reform: structural reform to restore competitiveness and growth, fiscal reform to restore sustainability of public finances, and repair and reform of the banking system. Italy and Spain have new leadership committed to restoring market confidence. In Italy, a country that ran primary surpluses for seventeen consecutive years preceding the financial crisis, the key challenge is to strengthen competitiveness and growth. After just a few months in office, Prime Minister Monti has is laying the groundwork for a more dynamic economy, with a first round of measures to liberalize the retail sector and create incentives for companies to increase investment and hire more women and youth. A second round, that includes liberalization of professions, transport, energy, and other sectors, has been submitted to parliament. Negotiations on labor reforms are ongoing.

Likewise, Spanish President Mariano Rajoy is moving aggressively to address Spain's vulnerabilities, including by undertaking a historic restructuring of its financial sector, which has reduced the number of savings banks to 15 from 45 and improved their institutional governance and framework. Spain's Cabinet recently approved a draft bill that obliges all levels of government to approve expenditure ceilings and debt targets, with fines for non-compliance, and introduces tougher monitoring of regions' fiscal situations.

Each of these countries face an extremely challenging agenda and completion will require determined efforts over a sustained period of time.

These efforts by individual countries are being reinforced across the euro area by broader economic governance reform. On December 9 of last year, Europe elaborated plans to strengthen the foundations of the euro area through a fiscal compact and stronger coordination of economic policies. Late last month, leaders from 25 of the 27 EU member states endorsed the agreement.

Second, European monetary and banking authorities have taken steps to provide strong assurances that European banks will have access to liquidity and build strong capital buffers. In recent months, the European Central Bank (ECB) has taken critical actions, including lowering interest rates, providing liquidity to banks and buying sovereign bonds in the secondary market. Last December, in the face of deterioration in bank liquidity conditions and with frontloaded bank debt amortizations on the horizon, the ECB introduced the three-year Long-Term Refinancing Operation (LTRO) and announced broader eligibility for collateral, which seems to have significantly eased bank funding pressures and tensions in sovereign debt markets. Meanwhile, the European Banking Authority has undertaken an effort designed to significantly strengthen bank capital buffers.

Discussions on a successor program to support Greek reform efforts are ongoing, as are discussions with private bondholders on a voluntary exchange. Since 2009, Greece has undertaken fiscal consolidation of approximately 5 percentage points of GDP. Greece has also implemented a reform of its pension system and a labor reform aimed at liberalizing wage negotiations and promoting more flexibility in employment schemes. But with a heavy debt burden and significant lack of competitiveness, Greece will need to sustain a challenging path of reforms for many years in order to restore growth and sustainability.

Finally, it is critical that the euro area continue its efforts to build a strong firewall to stem contagion and to ensure that sovereigns undertaking difficult fiscal and structural reforms have access to financing at sustainable rates. In December, European leaders agreed to establish a permanent crisis resolution fund, the European Stabilization Mechanism (ESM), by June –a year ahead of schedule. And they committed to assess the adequacy of resources in their firewall at their next summit in March.

The United States and our international partners stand with European leaders as they move to put in place a comprehensive solution. And we have welcomed the IMF's role in helping to contain the crisis and its impact on the U.S. recovery and global economy by providing advice and helping to design programs for the most vulnerable European countries, as well as providing a minority share of funding in certain circumstances. However, while the IMF should continue to play a constructive role in Europe, IMF resources cannot substitute for a strong and credible European firewall and response. The challenge Europe faces is within the capacity of the Europeans to manage and the Administration has been clear with our international partners that we are not seeking additional funding for the IMF.

By promoting greater stability and safeguarding against further deterioration of economic conditions, the IMF supports the global economy, and with that, U.S. growth, jobs, and exports. The IMF has played, and can continue to play, an important role in the European crisis response. With its wealth of experience and independent judgment, the IMF sets strong economic conditions that help return countries to sustainability. In this regard, the IMF has unparalleled credibility providing external assessments of reform programs. And through our role on the IMF board as the largest shareholder, the U.S. plays an important role shaping the terms and policies of adjustment programs. It is in our national interest to retain that leading influence in the IMF. In 2009 rapid Congressional support for IMF action helped stabilize the global recovery and ensured continued U.S. leadership in the institution.

The IMF has played this critical role in every major post-war financial crisis while consistently returning to the United States and other IMF members any resources –with interest—that it has temporarily drawn upon.

CONCLUSION

Europe is an important partner and ally strategically and economically. The euro-area crisis remains the foremost challenge to global growth, and to our domestic recovery. We will continue to actively engage with our European partners as they work to put in place a comprehensive solution to restore market confidence and ensure the health and resilience of the euro area. This is important to safeguard American jobs and protect our overall economic recovery.

In: Economic Crisis in the Eurozone ISBN: 978-1-62081-788-9
Editors: E. F. Young and T. D. Murphy

Chapter 8

TESTIMONY OF STEVEN B. KAMIN, DIRECTOR OF INTERNATIONAL FINANCE DIVISION. HEARING ON "EXAMINING THE EUROPEAN DEBT CRISIS AND ITS IMPLICATIONS"*

Thank you, Chairman Johnson, Ranking Member Shelby, and members of the Committee for inviting me today to talk about the economic situation in Europe and actions taken by the Federal Reserve in response to this situation.

For two years now, developments in Europe have played a critical role in shaping the tenor of global financial markets. The combination of high debts, large deficits, and poor growth prospects in several European countries using the euro has raised concerns about their fiscal sustainability. Such concerns were initially focused on Greece but have since spread to a number of other euro-area countries, leading to substantial increases in their sovereign borrowing costs. Pessimism about these countries' fiscal situation, in turn, has helped to undermine confidence in the strength of European financial institutions, increasing the institutions' borrowing costs and threatening to curtail their supply of credit. These developments have strained global financial markets and weighed on global economic activity.

In the past several months, European leaders have taken a number of policy steps that have helped reduce financial market stresses. In early December, the European Central Bank, or ECB, reduced its policy interest

* This is an edited, reformatted and augmented version of the testimony given on February 16, 2012 before the Senate Banking Committee.

rate, cut its reserve requirement, eased collateral rules for its lending, and, perhaps most important, began providing three-year loans to banks. Additionally, European leaders announced and have started to implement proposals to strengthen fiscal rules and European fiscal coordination, as well as to expand the euro-area financial backstop. These steps are positive developments and signify the commitment of European leaders to alleviate the crisis.

Since early December, borrowing costs for several vulnerable European governments have declined, funding pressures for European banks have eased, and the tone of investor sentiment has improved. However, financial markets remain under strain. Europe's authorities continue to face difficult challenges as they seek to stabilize their fiscal and financial situation, and it will be critical for them to follow through on their policy commitments in the months ahead.

Here at home, the financial stresses in Europe are undoubtedly spilling over to the United States by restraining our exports, weighing on business and consumer confidence, and adding to pressures on U.S. financial markets and institutions. Of note, foreign financial institutions, especially those in Europe, continue to find it difficult to fund themselves in dollars. A great deal of trade and investment the world over is financed in dollars, so many foreign financial institutions have heavy borrowing needs in our currency. These institutions also borrow heavily in dollars because they are active in U.S. markets, purchasing government and corporate securities and lending to households and firms. As concerns about the financial system in Europe mounted, many European banks faced a rise in the cost and a decline in the availability of dollar funding. Difficulty acquiring dollar funding by European and other financial institutions may ultimately make it harder and more costly for U.S. households and businesses to get loans. Moreover, these disruptions could spill over into the market for borrowing and lending in U.S. dollars more generally, raising the cost of funding for U.S. financial institutions. Although the breadth and size of all of these effects on the U.S. economy are difficult to gauge, it is clear that the situation in Europe poses a significant risk to U.S. economic activity and bears close watching.

Swap Lines with Other Central Banks

To address these potential risks to the United States, as described in an announcement on November 30, the Federal Reserve agreed with the

European Central Bank (ECB) and the central banks of Canada, Japan, Switzerland, and the United Kingdom to revise, extend, and expand its swap lines with these institutions.[1] The measures were taken to ease strains in global financial markets, which, if left unchecked, could significantly impair the supply of credit to households and businesses in the United States and impede our economic recovery. Thus far, such strains have been particularly evident in Europe, and these actions were designed to help prevent them from spilling over to the U.S. economy.

Three steps were described in the November 30 announcement. First, we reduced the pricing of drawings on the dollar liquidity swap lines. The previous pricing had been at a spread of 100 basis points over the overnight index swap rate.[2] We reduced that spread to 50 basis points. The lower cost to the ECB and other foreign central banks enabled them to reduce the cost of the dollar loans they provide to financial institutions in their jurisdictions. Reducing these costs has helped alleviate pressures in U.S. money markets generated by foreign financial institutions, strengthen the liquidity positions of European and other foreign institutions, and boost confidence at a time of considerable strain in international financial markets. Through all of these channels, the action should help support the continued supply of credit to U.S. households and businesses.

Second, we extended the authorization for these lines through February 1, 2013. The previous authorization had been through August 1, 2012. This extension demonstrated that central banks are prepared to work together for a sustained period, if needed, to support global liquidity conditions.

Third, we agreed to establish, as a precautionary measure, swap lines in the currencies of the other central banks participating in the announcement. (The Federal Reserve had established similar lines in April 2009, but they were not drawn upon and were allowed to expire in February 2010.) These lines would permit the Federal Reserve, if needed, to provide euros, Canadian dollars, Japanese yen, Swiss francs, or British pounds to U.S. financial institutions on a secured basis, much as the foreign central banks provide dollars to institutions in their jurisdictions now. U.S. financial institutions are not experiencing any foreign currency liquidity pressures at present, but we judged it prudent to make arrangements to offer such liquidity should the need arise in the future.

I would like to emphasize that information on the swap lines is fully disclosed on the Federal Reserve's website--through our weekly balance sheet release and other materials--and information on swap transactions each week is provided on the website of the Federal Reserve Bank of New York.[3]

I also want to underscore that these swap agreements are safe from the perspective of the Federal Reserve and the U.S. taxpayer, for five main reasons:

- First, the swap transactions themselves present no exchange rate or interest rate risk to the Fed. Because the terms of each drawing and repayment are set at the time that the draw is initiated, fluctuations in exchange rates and interest rates that may occur while the swap funds are outstanding do not alter the amounts eventually to be repaid.
- Second, each drawing on the swap line must be approved by the Federal Reserve, which provides the Federal Reserve with control over use of the facility by the foreign central banks.
- Third, the foreign currency held by the Federal Reserve during the term of the swap provides added security.
- Fourth, our counterparties in these swap agreements are the foreign central banks. In turn, it is they who lend the dollars they draw from the swap lines to private institutions in their own jurisdictions. The foreign central banks assume the credit risk associated with lending to these institutions. The Federal Reserve has had long and close relationships with these central banks, and our interactions with them over the years have provided a track record that justifies a high degree of trust and cooperation.
- Finally, the short tenor of the swap drawings, which have maturities of at most three months, also offers some protection in that positions could be wound down relatively quickly were it judged appropriate to do so.

The Federal Reserve has not lost a penny on any of the swap line transactions since these lines were established in 2007, even during the most intense period of activity at the end of 2008. Moreover, at the maturity of each swap transaction, the Federal Reserve receives the dollars it provided plus a fee. These fees add to overall earnings on Federal Reserve operations, thereby increasing the amount the Federal Reserve remits to taxpayers.

Conclusion

The changes in swap arrangements that I have discussed have had some positive effects on dollar funding markets. Since the announcement of the changes at the end of November, the outstanding amount of dollar funding through the swap lines has increased substantially, to more than $100 billion, and several measures of the cost of dollar funding have declined.

That being said, many financial institutions, especially those from Europe, continue to find it difficult and costly to acquire dollar funding, in large part because investors remain uncertain about Europe's economic and financial prospects. Ultimately, the easing of strains in U.S. and global financial markets will require concerted action on the part of European authorities as they follow through on their announced plans to address their fiscal and financial difficulties. The situation in Europe is continuously evolving. Thus, we are closely monitoring events in the region and their spillovers to the U.S. economy and financial system.

Thank you again for inviting me to appear before you today. I would be happy to answer any questions you may have.

End Notes

[1] See Board of Governors of the Federal Reserve System (2011), "Coordinated Central Bank Action to Address Pressures in Global Money Markets," press release, November 30, www. federalreserve.gov/newsevents/press/monetary/20111130a.htm. Similar announcements appeared on the web sites of the other participating central banks.

[2] The dollar overnight index swap rate is the fixed rate that one party agrees to pay in exchange for the average of the overnight federal funds rates over the life of the swap. As such, it is a measure of the average federal funds rate expected over the term of the swap.

[3] For the outstanding amount of dollar funding through the swap lines as it appears each week in the Federal Reserve balance sheet, see www.federalreserve.gov/releases/h41. For other relevant information and materials on the Federal Reserve's website, see www.federal reserve.gov/monetarypolicy/bst_liquidityswaps.htm. For weekly information on the Federal Reserve's swap transactions with other central banks, see www.newyorkfed.org/markets/ fxswap/fxswap.cfm. Finally, for copies of the agreements between the Federal Reserve and other central banks, as well as other information, see www. newyorkfed.org/markets/ liquidity_swap.html.

In: Economic Crisis in the Eurozone ISBN: 978-1-62081-788-9
Editors: E. F. Young and T. D. Murphy

Chapter 9

TESTIMONY OF BERT ELY. HEARING ON "WHAT THE EURO CRISIS MEANS FOR TAXPAYERS AND THE U.S. ECONOMY, PART 1"*

Mr. Chairman McHenry, Ranking Member Quigley, and members of the Subcommittee, I very much appreciate the opportunity to testify to you today about the Euro crisis and what it could mean for U.S. taxpayers and the U.S. economy. After briefly presenting my perspective on the economic situation in Europe as I viewed it yesterday morning when I submitted this written testimony, I will then speculate on ways in which the Euro crisis could impact taxpayers and the U.S. economy and discuss U.S. policy responses to a Euro crisis, including the November 30 announcement of new U.S. dollar swap arrangements between the Federal Reserve and five other central banks.[1]

THE ECONOMIC SITUATION IN EUROPE

I do not hold myself out an expert on the European economy but clearly it is facing serious economic problems including the survivability of the Euro, stresses within the European Union, and economic weaknesses throughout Europe. I will summarize key issues plaguing the European economy.

* This is an edited, reformatted and augmented version of the testimony given on December 15, 2011 before the House Committee on Oversight and Government Reform.

The Euro

Europe would not be experiencing its economic crisis had the Euro never been created or at least if the Euro zone had not been expanded to the number of countries it now has. Today, the Euro zone is a monetary union of 17 member countries of the 27-nation European Union (EU). The other ten EU members, notably the United Kingdom, Sweden, and Denmark, have elected to keep their own currencies rather than converting to the Euro. Two small but still significant European countries — Switzerland and Norway — have not joined the EU and therefore have retained their own currencies.

The fundamental problem with the 17-nation Euro zone is that it ties seventeen quite dissimilar economies to a common currency. While the total population of the Euro zone countries — 332 million — is somewhat greater than the current U.S. population — 313 million — and the GDP of the Euro zone approaches that of the United States, the Euro zone lacks the economic, cultural, and language integration that has long benefited the United States. The Euro zone's insufficient integration impairs the sustainability of the Euro zone as it is now constituted.

A key characteristic of a sustainable currency area (e.g., the United States, Canada, and Australia) is that there are minimal barriers to the movement of goods, services, and labor within the currency area. Put another way, a sustainable currency area is a free-trade area with a relatively unrestrained movement of goods, services, and labor so that market forces can lessen regional differences, in part by disciplining local and regional government policies which impede an area's economic competitiveness. The continuing shift of economic activity within the United States reflects the workings of those market forces.

Unfortunately, these keys to sustainability are not present in the Euro zone as it is now constituted. While the EU abolished internal tariffs, there still are many practical barriers to the movement of goods, services, and labor within the EU. While some of these barriers are informal — differences in language, culture, and attitudes — other barriers reflect the operation of national laws, notably labor laws that have not been harmonized within the Euro zone, much less across the entire EU. Arguably, the Euro subsidized the retention of national laws which impair the efficiency of industry in that country, and especially export-oriented industries — these countries have enjoyed low interest rates on their private-sector and public-sector debt. However, there is no free lunch — export goods produced in these countries have steadily lost international competitiveness. This has been especially true across the southern belt of the Euro zone — Greece, Italy, Portugal, Spain, and further north, in Ireland.

In many regards, the Euro, as a unit of account (e.g., dollar, pound, franc, mark, etc.), suffers the same weaknesses as the classical gold standard or any commodity standard (e.g., silver, copper, wampum, cigarettes, etc.) which ties several or many countries to a fixed relationship between the units of account of those countries. Because national economies evolve at different rates of economic growth and public-policy innovation (e.g., such as reducing labor-market rigidities or modernizing tax systems), economic tensions develop — the fixed relationships between units of account become increasingly difficult to maintain until a breaking point is reached and the fixed relationships are irretrievably broken. That is what happened in the early 1930s as various nations abandoned the gold standard (e.g. Britain in 1931 and the United States in 1933). The Euro faces the same threat, with Greece the most likely candidate to first abandon the Euro, returning to the drachma as its national currency.

Abandoning a commodity standard or a common currency effectively represents a shift from a fixed-exchange rate to a floating exchange rate for the country's currency. Almost certainly a new Greek drachma, a new Italian lira, or a new Spanish peseta would be worth less, relative to other currencies, than the Euro, which would make those countries' exports more competitive, to the extent that a potential competitive advantage was not wiped out by more costly imports and/or increased domestic inflation. The immediate effect of a country such as Greece shifting back to its old currency from the Euro would be comparable to a nation with its own currency devaluing that currency relative to other currencies. The country presumably also would become more attractive as a tourist destination, at least for budget-minded tourists.

In many ways, the Euro is comparable to a currency board, an arrangement in which a country ties the value of its unit of account to that of another country, usually a large country with a strong economy. In the Euro zone, the Euro can reasonably be viewed today as merely another name for the German mark. Also, a number of small countries effectively use the currency of a large country as its own currency. For example, Panama effectively uses the U.S. dollar as its currency; the U.S. dollar is legal tender in Panama. Ecuador similarly uses the U.S. dollar as its currency. Arguably, Greece effectively uses the German mark as its own currency. However, because the Greek economy has not kept up with the German economy, that linkage may no longer be sustainable, in which case Greece has no choice but to abandon the Euro.

Abandoning the Euro, though, would be quite painful for a country and its people and businesses, for two key reasons. First, debts such as mortgages and bonds denominated in Euros would have to be abrogated and rewritten in the new local currency to spare debtors from being crushed by repayment obligations in a now suddenly more expensive Euro. This abrogation would be comparable to what occurred in the United States after it abandoned the gold standard in 1993 — the Gold Reserve Act of 1934 abrogated the gold clause in all public and private contracts, a legislative act the U.S. Supreme Court upheld in 1935. One can readily wonder what steps creditors in the weak Euro countries are taking to protect themselves against a comparable abrogation.

Second, owners of Euros in the weak Euro nations, fearful of being forced to convert their Euros into their country's new, less valuable currency, appear to be shifting their Euros to banks in stronger Euro-zone countries, notably Germany, into other currencies, such as the Swiss Franc or the U.S. dollar, or into gold or other commodities. According to a recent *New York Times* article, Greeks have withdrawn almost 40 billion Euros from the Greek banking system over the last year, equal to about 17 percent of Greek GDP, including 14 billion Euros in September and October.[2] Such currency shifting further exacerbates the liquidity problems in the banks of the economically weak Euro-zone countries while reducing the banks' capacity to lend.

The recent last-ditch attempt to fix the Euro by amending the EU Treaty to impose greater fiscal discipline on the Euro zone, will not work, at least in the short term. First, even if the United Kingdom were to back away from its veto of the proposed treaty changes, it is questionable if voters in other nations which held a referendum about the treaty changes would support the changes. News reports yesterday indicated that there is growing resistance within some non-Euro zone EU countries to the proposed changes in the EU treaty.

Second, the fiscal problems in many Euro zone countries are so deeply embedded that they can not be fixed within a few years — it will be a decades-long process that will not move at a uniform pace throughout the Euro zone. Some of these deep-seated problems are discussed in the following sections of this testimony.

Excessive Public Debt Rapidly Expanding due to Huge Budget Deficits

Excessive public-sector debt is an underlying cause of the weakness in many Euro-zone countries. Worse, that debt is growing rapidly, relative to a country's GDP, due to annual budget deficits. Although the Maastricht Treaty, which created the EU in 1992, established ceilings of public-debt-to-GDP (60%) and annual budget deficits (3% of GDP) for EU members, those ceilings are essentially unenforceable, with the consequence that most EU countries now exceed the public-debt-to-GDP ceiling. According to IMF data, key Euro zone countries had the following public-debt-to-GDP ratios for 2010: Greece — 143%; Italy — 119%; Belgium — 97%; Ireland — 95%; Germany — 84%; France — 82%; and Netherlands — 64%. Of course, the United States does not look too good by this measure either — with a public-debt-to-GDP ratio of 94% for 2010.

The public debt problem in the Euro zone is worsening rapidly due to large government spending deficits, rising interest rates, and weak economies. According to Eurostat,[3] government *deficits* as a percent of GDP among select countries were as follows: Ireland — 31.3%; Greece — 10.6%; Portugal — 9.8%; Spain — 9.3%; France — 7.1%; Italy — 4.6%; and Germany — 4.3%. As debt piles up in these countries, due to these large deficits, interest rates are rising on public debt, which exacerbates their deficit and debt problems. Slow economic growth or worse, a European recession, will only make matters worse. Where it all ends is anyone's guess, but a fracturing of the Euro zone has become increasingly inevitable.

Efforts by the EU to hold itself together and to preserve the Euro led to the creation of the European Financial Stability Fund (EFSF) and the growing pressure on the European Central Bank (ECB) to become an even bigger purchaser of European government debt. However, the ECB does not have an unlimited capacity to finance EU governments — it is merely a vehicle for effectively redistributing to the EU weaker countries the creditworthiness of Europe's larger, stronger economies, notably Germany and to some extent, France. However, even Germany has its limits — economically and politically — as to the extent to which it can support the ECB and the EFSF in their efforts to help embattled nations work through their economic problems while struggling to stay in the Euro zone.

External assistance, though, cannot save the day for Europe. The IMF has limited resources since ultimately it is backed by increasingly indebted countries nor can Europe realistically look to surplus countries, notably China and Japan, for substantial funding assistance. The United States, with its substantial outstanding debt and huge budget deficits certainly cannot be tapped to help finance Europe, except for modest IMF contributions.

Restructuring sovereign debt, such as the "voluntary" 50% debt reduction proposed for Greek bonds, may become a necessity, but such debt restructurings could become classified as debt defaults under credit default swaps (CDS), which would trigger huge losses under those CDS contracts for banks, insurance companies, and other parties who provided default insurance on sovereign debt. Those CDS losses would topple dominoes throughout Europe, and beyond. Growing uncertainty among investors about their ability to collect on CDS they purchased on sovereign debt that later defaults is leading to higher interest rates on sovereign debt, further exacerbating the government deficit and debt problem in the Euro zone. Europe's turkeys, in the form of years of excessive government spending, are finally coming home to roost, and they may stay a while.

Banks Weakened by Excessive Holdings of Sovereign Debt

European banks are substantial investors in sovereign debt, specifically bonds issued by their home country as well as by other EU countries. There are a variety of institutional and structural reasons that vary from country to country as to why European banks are substantial investors in bonds issued by EU nations, but the Basel risk-based capital standards, which have treated sovereign debt as riskless, certainly increased the incentive for banks to hold sovereign debt.

Unfortunately, there is no such thing as riskless sovereign debt, as Europe is now learning However, the damage is done, through losses on sovereign debt caused by the recognition of a loss when the debt is sold for less than book value, the debt defaults, or is restructured. Banks also face losses to the extent that they will have to pay out for losses incurred under CDS contracts, should events of default under those contracts ever be declared. All of these losses will deplete the banks' equity capital, rendering some EU banks insolvent.

As a result of recent stress tests, many EU banks clearly need to raise fresh equity capital, but many of them will not be able to demonstrate the going-forward earning power needed to attract that capital. What then? Will undercapitalized or insolvent European banks be allowed to continue operating, as the United States permitted hundreds of insolvent S&Ls to stay open during the 1980s, thereby making a mockery of the Basel III risk-based capital standards now being phased in? Or will individual nations or the EU launch TARP-like programs to invest taxpayer monies in the weak banks, hoping that the banks eventually will be restored to sufficient profitability so that they can raise fresh private-sector equity capital in the capital markets?

One can easily envision many marketplace distortions in the European financial markets over the next few years as the EU and its member countries deal with their banking problems, problems that could grow worse before they get better, should Europe slide into a full-fledged recession. How those distortions spill over into the United States is a question Congress, banking regulators, and the U.S. financial-services industry need to address.

Demographics — An Aging Population and the Entitlements Challenge

A key driver of the EU's fiscal woes is the welfare state, and especially its public pension schemes. This problem parallels the U.S. entitlements challenge of dealing with an aging population and more specifically a growing portion of the population who is retired and drawing a pension, sometimes at a high level relative to income earned during working years. Given the political challenge of extending the retirement age and/or reducing retirement benefits, the entitlement obligations now bearing down on the Euro zone countries suggest that these countries will experience great difficulty in eliminating their budget deficits, or at least trimming them substantially so they can eventually reduce their public-debt-to-GDP ratio. Who will continue to buy the debt of these countries, especially of the most indebted ones, and at what interest rate is at the heart of Europe's fiscal challenges.

Labor Market Rigidities and Other Economic Impediments

Another long-term economic challenge facing the Euro-zone countries are labor-market rigidities, which vary from country to country, reinforced by strong labor unions. These rigidities have two key negative effects. First, they increase the difficulty of employers adjusting to changing economic conditions by laying off employees, restructuring jobs, relocating factories, and other labor-related actions which enable employers to improve labor productivity and therefore their competitiveness. This is an especially challenging circumstance in the weaker countries already having to function with a stronger currency than they would have if they had not converted to the Euro. Put another way, implicit in converting to the Euro is adopting those public policies, including labor policies, which will enable that country to compete successfully against other Eurozone countries in terms of exports as well as import substitution. It is not clear how well that obligation is understood within the Euro zone.

Second, Europe lacks the labor mobility comparable to what has long existed in the United States. To some extent this lack of mobility is a function of language and cultural differences among the Euro zone countries but national labor laws also are widely viewed as impediments to labor mobility. Consequently, pockets of unemployment persist, with their attendant social-welfare costs which adds further to national budget deficits.

A host of other public-policy issues arise in the weaker Euro zone economies that impair their ability to compete and prosper in the Euro zone. Tax systems and effective tax collection are often cited as a contributing cause of government budget deficits, notably in Greece and Italy. Impediments against entrepreneurial initiatives and a lack of venture capital also can be cited. Bottom line, the weaker Euro zone countries have a lot of work to do to enhance their ability to stay in the Euro zone. How many will succeed in doing so is huge question, with global implications.

How a Euro Crisis Could Impact the U.S. Economy and U.S. Taxpayers

A Euro crisis would slow European economic activity, possibly throwing the EU back into recession. Hopefully that would be as bad as it would get. However, if enough dominoes toppled within the Euro zone, Europe could experience a deep, prolonged recession, or worse. Given the highly interconnected nature of the global economy, U.S. exports to Europe would decline, which would have negative effects on the U.S. economy. To the extent that a European recession triggered a global economic slowdown, which is quite possible, then U.S. economic activity would slow even more, with the U.S. possibly falling into a recession as the European economy sorts itself out. The U.S. unemployment rate surely would rise.

Clearly a slowing U.S. economy would increase the already enormous U.S. budget deficit as tax receipts declined and federal spending related to unemployment rose. There also might be new rounds of stimulus spending. Consequently, the U.S. economy would look more and more like the most troubled European countries — huge budget deficits and a rising debt-to-GDP percentage. It will not be a pretty picture.

POSSIBLE U.S. POLICY RESPONSES TO A EURO CRISIS

Unfortunately, the United States has few options for dealing with the Euro crisis — either before or after the Euro zone begins to crumble. At the present time, the best the United States can do is continue urging the EU to work aggressively in addressing its problems in order to hold the Euro zone together as best it can. In particular, the United States should encourage the weaker Euro zone countries to continue addressing their structural problems so as to improve their competitiveness, thereby improving the likelihood that they can remain in the Euro zone. Further expansion of the Euro zone should be questioned while there is so much uncertainty about the future of the Euro.

Given its financial weaknesses, the federal government certainly should not supply any direct financial assistance to help preserve the Euro, such as buying the debt of any of the Euro zone countries. However, I am supportive of the U.S. dollar swap arrangements recently entered into with five other central banks, as noted above. These arrangements provide liquidity, in the form of U.S. dollars, which will help to keep the European financial system functioning while the EU works through its problems.

Four of those central banks — the Bank of Canada, the Bank of England, the Bank of Japan, and the Swiss National Bank — are outside the Euro zone. Given the terms of the swap arrangements, I see no taxpayer risk, as a practical matter, with these four swap arrangements. Swap deals such as these have been done for decades without any loss. Arguably there is a slight taxpayer risk in any swap arrangement with the ECB — it might not return all the dollars it borrowed upon the termination of the swap. However, that is such a slight risk relative to the importance of lending dollars to the ECB that I do not worry about it.

Above all, the United States should take the Euro crisis as yet another wake-up call that the United States must put its economic house in order by trimming budget deficits, gradually reducing its debt-to-GDP ratio, increasing the domestic savings rate, reducing the magnitude of the United States' net-debtor position with the rest of the world, addressing the entitlements challenges posed by Social Security and Medicare, improving its tax system by removing disincentives for savings and investing, and increasingly the economy's international competitiveness. This is an enormous, difficult, and politically challenging task, but it is one that we as a country must undertake, for we are not immune from being laid low by excessive debt and deficit spending, as has Greece and soon possibly other Euro zone countries.

Thank you for this opportunity to testify this morning. I welcome your questions.

End Notes

[1] The Bank of Canada, the Bank of England, the Bank of Japan, the European Central Bank, and the Swiss National Bank.

[2] Thomas, Landon, "Pondering a Dire Day: Leaving the Euro," *The New York Times*, December 12, 2011, pg. B 1.

[3] http://epp.eurostatec.europa.eu/portal/page/portal/eurostat/home/

In: Economic Crisis in the Eurozone ISBN: 978-1-62081-788-9
Editors: E. F. Young and T. D. Murphy

Chapter 10

TESTIMONY OF JACOB FUNK KIRKEGAARD. HEARING ON "THE EUROPEAN DEBT CRISIS: STRATEGIC IMPLICATIONS FOR THE TRANSATLANTIC ALLIANCE"*

Senator Shaheen, members of the subcommittee. It is a pleasure to testify before you today on the European Debt Crisis and its strategic implications for the transatlantic alliance.

The European debt crisis is characterized by an extreme degree of complexity, as the correct diagnosis is not one, but at least four deep, overlapping and mutually reinforcing crises – a crisis of institutional design, a fiscal crisis, a crisis of competitiveness, and a banking crisis.

None of the four crises can be solved in isolation and no single comprehensive solution to end the crisis promptly is available to EU policymakers, meaning the drawn-out inconclusive crisis containment efforts witnessed in Europe since early 2010 will continue.

At their summit last week, euro area leaders agreed on a new set of measures, which while inadequate in scope to end the crisis and calm financial market volatility will help militate against a new dramatic economic deterioration in Europe. The risk of catastrophic spillovers from Europe to the U.S. and global economy has therefore been reduced.

The euro area has agreed a voluntary bond swap agreement with private holders of Greek government debt resulting in a 50 percent reduction in the nominal debt value. This is an urgently needed measure, which however will

* This is an edited, reformatted and augmented version of the testimony given on November 2, 2011 before the Senate Foreign Relations Committee.

not independently restore Greek fiscal solvency. Meanwhile, as concerns over fiscal sustainability in the euro area stretches also to Italy, a country "too big to bailout", the principal challenge is how to avoid contagion and how to ring-fence Greece so as to avoid a generalized undermining of the "risk free status" of euro area government debt.

To achieve this goal, substantial financial support will in the years ahead have to be made available to Greece, as well as Ireland and Portugal. Such resources should overwhelmingly come from the euro area, with a component provided by the IMF. Ultimately though euro area fiscal stability will only be achieved through the longer-term domestic consolidation and reform efforts particularly in Italy.

The Greek debt swap is a voluntary transaction which looks unlikely to trigger sovereign default swaps. Apart from the superficial political pride available to European leaders from being able rhetorically to deny that a euro area default has taken place, a potential short-term source of dislocation in the financial markets has hereby been removed, as – although the net outstanding Greek CDS contract value amount to less than $4bn – little is known about the extent of individual, including U.S. financial institutions' gross CDS exposures.

However, the lack of payout after a 50 percent reduction in debt may ultimately lead to the demise of the sovereign CDS product class for at least industrialized nations. Financial markets will be certain to in the future doubt whether any advanced economy sovereign debt restructuring will trigger CDS protection. Given the multiple hedging purposes for sovereign CDS, this may ironically lead in increased financial market volatility in the future, including here in the United States.

Euro area leaders secondly agreed to raise the capital requirements in banks to 9 percent core tier 1 equity and adjust for the effects of market prices of sovereign debt. This is a helpful further step, which will help insulate also U.S. financial institutions against the risk of sudden bank collapses in Europe, but will not make Europe's banking system "stable and well capitalized". Substantially more new capital and an end to the solvency concerns surrounding several euro area sovereigns themselves will be required to restore market confidence in the stability of the European banking system.

Thirdly, euro area leaders agreed on two options to boost the financial firepower of the European Financial Stability Facility (EFSF). Both are, however, are almost certain to fail. Option one, "*to provide credit enhancement to new debt issued by Member States*[1]" is meaningless from a systemic euro area stability point of view. When the overlap between the insurer and the insured is as big as in the euro area, the beneficial financial effects will be minimal.

Option two foresees the creation of special purpose investment vehicles open to investments from "*private and public financial institutions and investors*". However, few if any such investors exist with the willingness and ability to invest the hundreds of billions of euros required to make a material difference for European financial stability. China will not bail Europe out and certainly, it would not be prudent use of U.S. taxpayers' money to contribute, just as the statutes of the IMF in all probability will prevent it from participating.

Fortunately though this does not matter, as the EFSF's principal purpose is political not financial. The two EFSF options described are a smokescreen created to provide political cover for the European Central Bank (ECB) to remain directly involved in the European crisis stabilization measures. This is critical, as only the ECB commands the resources to stabilize Europe.

Europe is America's largest trade and investment partner and extensive cross-ownership of large financial institutions exist. It is consequently inescapable that the U.S. domestic economy will experience a further negative external shock from any rapid deterioration of the European debt crisis.

However, the possible direct actions by U.S. policymakers have been limited by the fact that it is, despite increasing global spillover potential, still at heart a domestic economic crisis inside another sovereign jurisdiction. The ability of the U.S. government to bilaterally affect the outcome of the European debt crisis is consequently and appropriately limited.

Yet, the U.S. government representatives have since the beginning of the euro area crisis exercised important indirect pressure through multilateral channels and especially the IMF and the G-20 to expedite the European crisis resolution process and push it in generally beneficial directions.

The debt crisis will lead to substantial changes in European political, economic and defense potential. The crisis will with certainty lead to a more institutionally integrated euro area, potentially enabling the more coordinated projection of the continent's remaining capabilities, potentially creating an enhanced European partnership role for the U.S. The fact that the United Kingdom is unlikely to be part of a deeper integration of the euro area will however especially from the perspective of the United States be a complicating factor.

The multifaceted character of the European crisis ensures that it will only be solved through a lengthy and volatile process. Yet ultimately Europe's crisis can and will be solved through the use of overwhelmingly European financial resources.

I thank you for the opportunity to appear before the Subcommittee today and look forward to answering any questions you might have.

The remainder of my written testimony provides additional background information concerning the complex origin of the European debt crisis.

THE ORIGIN OF THE EURO AREA'S FOUR DIFFERENT CRISES, THEIR OVERLAPS AND MUTUAL REINFORCEMENT

The euro area crisis has gradually since May 2010 taken center-place in an increasingly volatile global economy. It has become evident that the crisis consists of four distinct, though frequently overlapping and mutually reinforcing crises; 1) A design crisis, as the euro area from its creation in the 1990s has lacked crucial institutions to ensure financial stability during a crisis; 2) A fiscal crisis centered in Greece, but present across the southern euro area and Ireland; 3) A competitiveness crisis manifest in large and persistent pre-crisis current account deficits in the euro area periphery and even larger intra-euro area current account imbalances; and 4) A banking crisis first visible in Ireland, but spreading throughout euro area via accelerating concerns over sovereign solvencies.

The Euro Area Design Challenge

The concrete thinking about an economic and monetary union (EMU) in Europe goes back to 1970, when the *Werner Report*[2] laid out a detailed three stage plan for the establishment of EMU in Europe by 1980. Members of the European Community would gradually increase coordination of economic and fiscal policies, while reducing exchange rate fluctuations and finally fixing these irrevocably. The collapse of the Bretton Woods system and the first oil crisis in the early 1970s caused the Werner Report proposals to be abandoned.

By the mid-1980s, following the 1979 creation of the European Monetary System and the initiation of Europe's internal market, European policymakers again took up the idea of EMU. The *Delors Report*[3] from 1989 envisioned the achievement of EMU by 1999, moving gradually (again in three stages) towards closer economic coordination among the EU members, with binding constraints on member states' national budgets, and a single currency with an independent European Central Bank (ECB).

While Europe's currency union therefore has lengthy historical roots, it was an unforeseen shock – German reunification in October 1990–that provided the political impetus for the creation of the Maastricht Treaty[4], which in 1992 provided the legal foundation and detailed design for today's euro area. With the historical parity in Europe between (West) Germany and France no longer a political and economic reality, French president Francois Mitterrand and German Chancellor Helmut Kohl launched the EMU process as a principally political project to irrevocably join the French, German and other European economies together in an economic and monetary union and cement European unity.

This political imperative for launching the euro by 1999, however, frequently facilitated that politically necessary compromises, rather than theoretically sound and rigorous rules and regulations made up the institutional framework for the euro.

While the earlier Werner and Delors reports discussing the design of EMU had been explicit about the requirement to compliment a European monetary union (e.g. the common currency) with a European economic union complete with binding constraints on member states' behavior, political realities in Europe made this goal unattainable within the timeframe dictated by political leaders following German reunification.

The continued principal self-identification among Europeans as first and foremost residents of their home country[5], i.e. Belgians, Germans, Poles, Italians etc., made the collection of direct taxes to fund a large centralized European budget implausible. The frequently discussed relatively high willingness of Europeans to pay taxes does not "extend to Brussels". The designers of the euro area was consequently compelled to create the common currency area without a sizable central fiscal authority with the ability to counter regional specific (asymmetric) economic shocks or re-instill confidence in private market participants in the midst of a crisis – like the one the euro area is currently experiencing.

Similarly, the divergence in the economic starting points among the politically prerequisite "founding members" of the euro area moreover made the imposition of firm, objective fiscal criteria for membership in the euro area politically impossible. The Maastricht Treaty in principle included at least two hard "convergence criteria" for euro area membership – the so-called "reference values" of 3 percent general government annual deficit limit and 60 percent general government gross debt limit[6]. However, in reality these threshold values were anything but fixed, as the Maastricht Treaty Article 104c stated that countries could exceed the 3 percent deficit target, if "*the ratio has declined substantially and continuously and reached a level that comes close to the reference value*", or "*excess over the reference value is only exceptional and temporary and the ratio remains close to the reference value*". Euro area countries could similarly exceed the 60 percent gross debt target, provided that "*the ratio is sufficiently diminishing and approaching the reference value at a satisfactory pace*".

In other words, it was a wholly political decision whether a country could become a member of the euro area or not, and had relatively less to do with the fundamental economic strengths and weaknesses of the country in question. As it was politically inconceivable to launch the euro without Italy, the third largest economy in continental Europe, or Belgium, home of the European capital Brussels, both countries became members despite in 1997-98 having gross debt levels of almost twice the reference value of 60 percent (Figure 1).

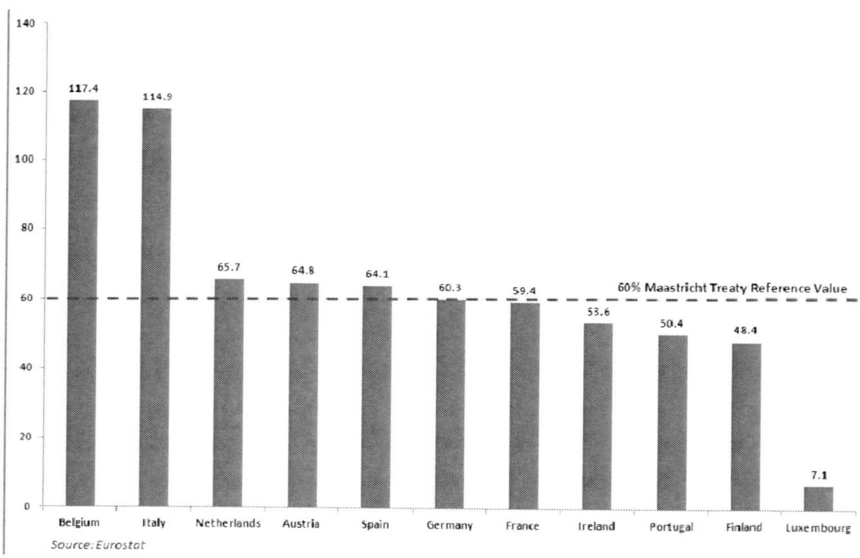

Figure 1. General Government Gross Debt 1998, 11 Original Euro Area Members, Percent of GDP.

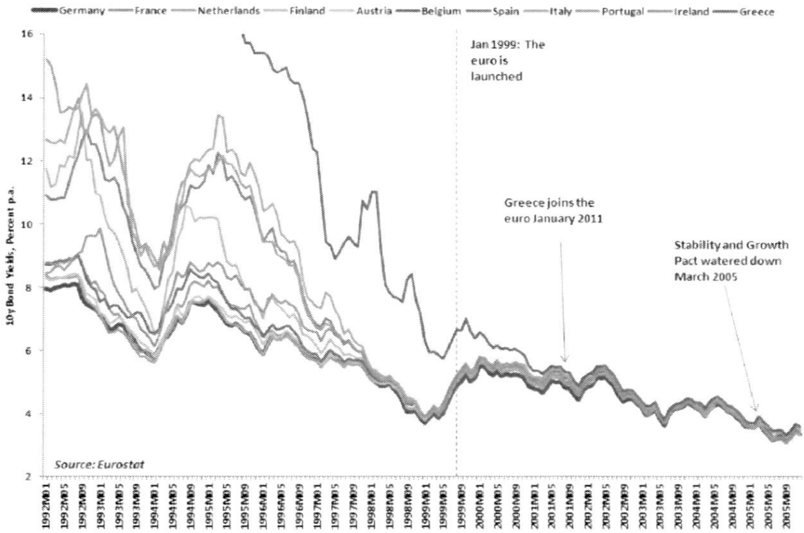

Figure 2. 10y Bond Rates among Euro Area members Jan 1992-Dec 2005.

As a result, Europe's monetary union was launched in 1999 comprising of a set of countries that were far more diverse in their economic fundamentals and far less economically integrated than had been envisioned in the earlier Werner and Delors reports. Yet, not only did European political leaders proceed with the launch of the euro with far more dissimilar countries than what economic theory would have predicted feasible, shortly after the launch of the euro, they went further and undermined the remaining credibility of the rules-based framework for the coordination of national fiscal policies in the euro area.

Building on the euro area convergence criteria, the Stability and Growth Pact (SGP) was intended to safeguard sound public finances, prevent individual euro area members from running unsustainable fiscal policies and thus guard against moral hazard by enforcing budget discipline. However, faced themselves with breaching the 3 percent deficit limit in 2002-2004, France and Germany pushed through a watering down of the SGP rules in March 2005[7] that, as in the Maastricht Treaty itself, introduced sufficient flexibility into the interpretation of SGP that its enforcement became wholly political and with only limited reference to objective economic facts. Individual euro members subsequently failed to restore the long-term sustainability of their finances during the growth years before the global financial crisis began.

By 2005 the euro area was as a result of numerous shortcuts taken to achieve and sustain a political goal, a common currency area consisting of a very dissimilar set of countries, without a central fiscal agent, without any credible enforcement of budget discipline or real deepening economic convergence. Initially, however, none of these danger signs mattered, as the financing costs in private financial markets of all euro area members quickly fell towards the traditionally low interest rates of Germany (Figure 2).

It is beyond this testimony to speculate about the causes of this lasting colossal mispricing of credit risk in the euro area sovereign debt markets by private investors in the first years after the introduction of the euro. The financial effects of this failure on the other hand were obvious, as euro area governments and private investors were able to finance themselves at historically low (often significantly negative real) interest rates seemingly irrespective of their economic fundamentals. Large public and private debt overhangs were correspondingly built up in the euro area during the first years of the euro area and in the run up to the global financial crisis in 2008. Financial markets' failure to properly assess the riskiness of different euro area countries papered over these issues until the global financial crisis finally struck.

The euro area institutional design has in essence been that of a "fair weather currency", with no central institutions capable of compelling the member states to act in unison. As a new, untested and severely under-institutionalized entity, the euro area has had no capacity to act forcefully during the current crisis or restore confidence among private businesses and consumers. Unless that changes, the euro area will be unable to exit the current crisis.

European policymakers therefore today are faced with the acute challenge of correcting the design flaws in the euro area institutions that their predecessors in their quest to quickly realize a political vision for Europe helped create. The euro area needs a new rule book. Leaders must in the midst of this crisis craft a new set of euro area institutions that for the first time provide the common currency with binding fiscal rules for its member states, and a centralized fiscal entity capable of acting in a crisis on behalf of the euro area as a whole. This will require the transfer of sovereignty from individual member states to the supra-national euro area level considerably beyond what has previously occurred in the EU.

The Euro Area Fiscal Challenge

The euro area fiscal crisis is concentrated in Greece, which according to the latest IMF/EC/ECB estimates will have a general government debt surpassing 180 percent of GDP by 2012. Despite Greece's IMF program and associated financial support from the EU and IMF since May 2010, the country is at this point clearly not able to repay all its creditors in full and has to restructure its government debt. Greece will consequently be the first ever euro area country and first OECD member since shortly after World War 2 forced to restructure its sovereign debt.

Portugal and Ireland are currently subject to IMF programs, too, but in contrast to Greece have successfully implemented their program commitments to this date[8]. Through continued strong reform implementation and access to financial assistance from the EU and IMF in the years ahead, it looks still potentially feasible for Portugal and Ireland to in the medium-term restore their access to private financial markets at sustainable interest rates.

However, as illustrated in figure 3, the cost of financing for Spain and Italy has also risen substantially in recent month with secondary 10y bond market yields currently between 5.5 and 6 percent. Unlike, however, the three smaller euro area countries with IMF programs, Spain and Italy are economies of a size that makes them "too big to bailout" for the euro area, even with IMF help. The fact that financial markets have begun to doubt the fiscal sustainability of "too big to bailout" members of the euro area is at the heart of the euro area policy makers' fiscal challenge.

The key link between Greece and Spain and Italy is the issue of "contagion"[9], i.e. a situation in which instability in a specific asset markets or institutions is transmitted to one or more other specific such asset markets or institutions. Inside a currency union like the euro area, where the central bank is legally barred from guaranteeing all the sovereign debts of individual member states[10] and the for political reasons each sovereign members' debts remains distinct[11], yet the debt is denominated in the same currency and governed by at least some common institutions, the phenomenon of contagion has particular force. If private investors begin to fear that a precedent will be set inside the euro area with the imposition of haircuts on Greek sovereign debt, they will assess the riskiness of other euro area members' sovereign debt differently once the "risk free status" of euro area sovereign debt has been impaired. The large increases in the interest rates on Italian and Spanish government debt seen immediately following the July 21st, 2011 EU Council decision to first introduce haircuts on Greek government debt looks, in the absence of simultaneous new bad economic news released from the two countries, to be largely due to contagion.

Given the high public and private debt levels built up before the global financial crisis in Spain and Italy, the sudden emergence of contagion and associated reprising by private investors of the riskiness of these two countries has the potential initiate destabilizing self-fulfilling interest rate-solvency spirals. Contagion from Greece causes Italian interest rates to go up, which given Italy's high existing debt levels adds materially to the interest burden, necessitating further austerity measures, further reducing economic growth in the short-term, leading to lower government revenues and increased financial market concerns, again increasing both the Italian government deficit and interest burden. The presence of contagion inside a currency union, where many individual members have high debt levels consequently have to potential of turning what might previously have been stable and sustainable high debt burdens into unstable unsustainable debt burdens.

The unique degree of independence of the ECB adds a further complication to such contagion inside the euro area. Its independence derives from Article 282 of the EU Treaty[12], which states that the central bank "*shall be independent in the exercise of its powers and in the management of its finances. Union institutions, bodies, offices and agencies, and the governments of the Member States shall respect that independence.*" With Treaty-defined independence, the ECB is more akin to a Supreme Court than a central bank in the mold of the U.S. Federal Reserve, whose independence is derived from the Federal Reserve Act passed by Congress (which Congress expressly reserves the right to amend, alter, or repeal[13]). The ECB has no political masters and the EU Treaty moreover bars bar elected officials from criticizing its decisions.

In a sovereign and financial crisis, such total central bank independence might actually hinder the restoration of market confidence, because it might further undermine investors' trust in the solvency of a government that does not ultimately control its own central bank, lacks its own currency, and thus has no ultimate lender of last resort. The European Treaty's Article 123 forbids the ECB to extend credit to member states, preventing it from issuing any blanket guarantees for their sovereign debt. Due to the complete independence of the ECB and the restrictions the EU Treaty places on it, the euro area thus lacks an important confidence boosting measure in the face of contagion.

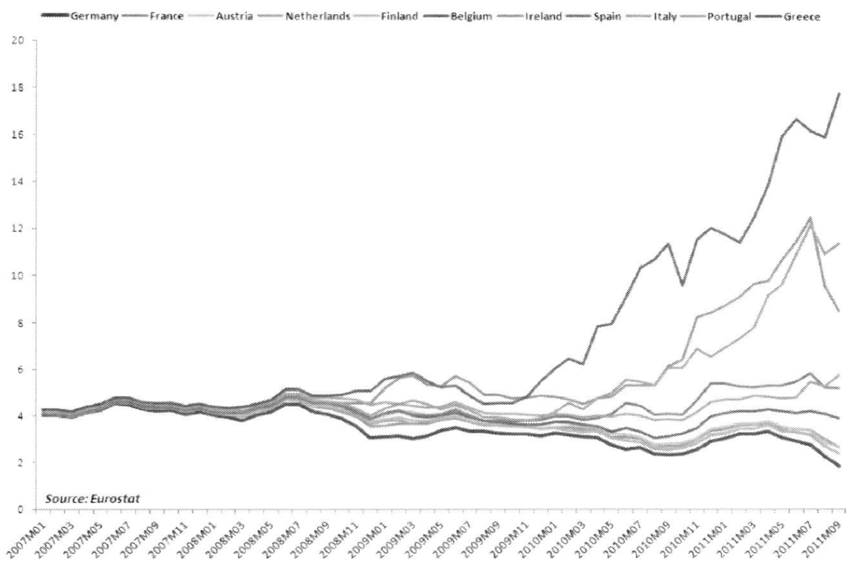

Figure 3. 10y Bond Rates among Euro Area members Jan 2007-Oct 2011.

On the other hand, the ECB's independence and status as the only pan-euro area institution capable of direct forceful action to calm global financial markets bestows upon the ECB's governing council a degree of leverage over elected officials in this crisis not seen elsewhere in the world. This gives the ECB leadership the ability to engage in horse-trading with democratically elected governments behind closed doors, where it can quietly demand that government leaders implement far-reaching reforms. A clear example of this came in August 2011 just ahead of the ECB's initiation of emergency support purchases of Italian government debt. The sitting and incoming presidents of the ECB wrote bluntly to Italian Prime Minister Silvio Berlusconi, stating that "the [ECB] Governing Council considers that pressing action by the Italian authorities is essential to restore the confidence of investors[14]" followed by a list of more than ten specific required reforms to be implemented by the Italian government.

The degree of independence and influence of the ECB matters for the attempts to find an expeditions solution to the euro area fiscal crisis, as it is actually not in the ECB's interest to act too decisively to immediately try to end any contagion or the crisis more broadly. It is not that the ECB cannot step in. There is no asset it cannot buy, if the governing council agrees. The strategy of allowing financial market mayhem to pressure European governments is therefore less risky than it seems. Ultimately, the ECB has the means to calm markets down but its intention is to do so only to avoid absolute disaster.

A sweeping preemptive "helping hand to euro area governments" under speculative attack would from the perspective of the ECB be counterproductive, as it would relieve pressure on governments to reform. The ECB's game is thus not to end the crisis at all costs as soon as possible, but to act deliberatively to cajole governments into implementing the crisis solutions it wants. The market volatility seen accelerating in recent months becomes something not to be avoided, but to use as a club against recalcitrant and reform-resistant euro area leaders.

European policymakers therefore today are faced with the acute challenge of enabling Greece to restructure its unsustainable sovereign debt, while at the same time ensuring that such an event has no precedent-setting effects inside the euro area and that contagion among sovereign debt markets consequently is contained. Ring-fencing Greece geographically and in the time dimension (i.e. assuring that Greece will only ever go through a single one-off sovereign debt restructuring) will require further financial assistance in the coming years be provided to Greece itself, as well as Portugal and Ireland. The sizable majority of this support must sensible come from the rest of the euro area, with some continued financial participation also of the IMF.

In addition to further restrict contagion, euro area leaders must device a method which can provide a degree of preemptive financial support to "too big to bailout" euro area members and potentially lower their primary bond market cost of finance. This is the key aspect of the current debate surrounding how to utilize the €440bn European Financial Stability Facility (EFSF) most effectively. However, given the constraints on and reluctance of the ECB to participate directly in any such financial support (though for instance providing leverage to the EFSF) to large non-IMF program countries, the resources available to euro area leaders will be constrained. Any financial benefits to large beneficiary countries like Spain and Italy from new euro area measures will moreover be relatively limited, due to the large weight inside the euro area itself of the beneficiary countries themselves. Irrespective of the ultimate format chosen by euro area leaders, the "correlation between benefactors and beneficiaries" will be so large that the financial advantage will be relatively modest. There will be no euro area "bazooka" created from the EFSF.

Ultimately, the euro area will have to rely on its large members to "bail themselves out" through a lengthy period of fiscal consolidation. Financial markets are unlikely to be satisfied with this outcome, and while the ECB will continue to act as a conditional final defender of financial stability in the euro area, heightened levels of uncertainty and volatility will remain a feature of the euro area sovereign debt and other asset markets several years ahead.

The Euro Area Competitiveness Challenge

The euro area was wrought by merging together in a single currency a number of highly divergent European economies, and for reasons of political expediency any binding political euro area rules and intrusive regulations that could during the euro's first decade have forced a real economic convergence to occur among divergent euro area members were abandoned. Cushioned by the seemingly secure access to cheap financing once inside the euro area, most member states moreover scaled back the implementation of structural reforms of their national economies[15].

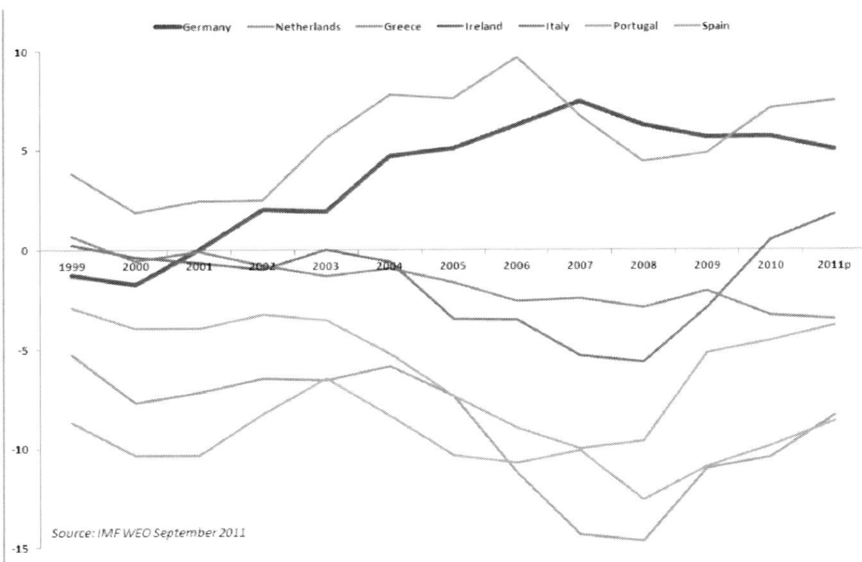

Figure 4. Current Account Balances 1999-2011p, Select Euro Area Members, Percent of GDP.

The principal exception was Germany, which in the years immediately after the euro introduction implemented a series of far reaching reforms of especially its labor markets and pension system. Consequently, Europe's traditionally strongest and most competitive economy during the first decade of the euro area gradually pulled itself even further ahead of most of the other members of the common currency. A persistent pattern inside the euro area consequently became the widening current account imbalances with Germany and other Northern members running surpluses and especially the Southern peripheral members running deficits (figure 4).

Financing their large external deficits posed few obstacles for peripheral countries prior to the global financial crisis, even as it became clearer that the inflows of foreign capital were increasingly channeled towards financing speculative real estate investments, rather than adding to new productive asset investments. With the disappearance of foreign private capital following the onslaught of the global financial crisis, peripheral euro area deficit countries and their banks suddenly found themselves instead overwhelmingly dependent on financial support from the ECB. However, while such central support will be continuous inside any functioning currency union, a longer-term requirement for peripheral euro area nations to regain competitiveness and restore external balance (or surplus) remains[16]. Without improving external competitiveness and increasing exports/reducing imports, the euro area periphery will not during their current prolonged period of fiscal consolidation be able to restore domestic economic growth.

Inside a currency union without the ability to devalue their currency against major trading partners, peripheral euro area members, however, do not have access to the traditionally fastest and most effective way through which a country can regain external competitiveness[17]. Consequently, the euro area peripheral countries only have means at their disposal to increase the competitiveness that might be effective in a longer-term framework. Such measures include numerous traditional "supply-side structural reforms" of especially peripheral euro area labor markets, where the often legally sanctioned coercive power of labor unions, the rigidity of collective bargaining agreements and automatic wage indexation to the public sector must be curtailed. Nominal wage levels at the firm level must be brought into line with productivity, an effort which in numerous instances will lead to nominal wage cuts.

European policymakers face a competitiveness challenge today in which the precise requirements of the euro area periphery to regain their external competitiveness and for the euro area as a whole to limit intra-euro area imbalances will vary depending on individual country circumstances and require additional measures in surplus countries (such as Germany), too. It is furthermore evident that available policy options inside a currency union are of a structural reform character. Such reforms can only hope to be effective in raising competitiveness and potential economic growth rates in the medium term, and will indeed in the short term, though for instance required nominal wage declines, hurt economic growth.

The Euro Area Banking Crisis

The first manifestations of a banking crisis in the euro area in Ireland in 2008 had relatively few pan-euro area elements about it. The Irish real estate boom was clearly supported by the record low negative real interest rates in the country following the introduction of the euro (figure 5), but the 2008 collapse of the Irish banking sector and subsequent required rescue of the Irish government by the EU and IMF was overwhelmingly due to domestic Irish domestic factors and failures[18]. That on the other hand is not true of the most recent volatility to affect the euro area banking system.

Several systematic ailments that plaque the euro area banking system are illustrated in table 1; First of all, the euro area's banking system is very large relative to the size of the overall home economies with average euro area financial institutions' gross debt equal to 143 percent of GDP (U.S. equal 94 percent). Secondly, euro area bank leverage is very high at tangible assets at 26 times common equity (U.S. level is at 12 times); and thirdly, euro area banks tend to own a lot of the debt issued by their own governments (something U.S. banks do to a much smaller degree).

The sheer size of the euro area banking system makes it – as illustrated in Ireland in 2008-10 – problematic for individual already indebted euro area governments to credibly issue guarantees to stand behind their domestic banks in a crisis. This issue is aggravated by the low level of common equity (core tier 1) capital in the euro area banks. With low private shareholder risk capital levels in euro area banks, euro area governments risks being frequently called upon to rescue domestic banks as only a thin layer of private equity capital is available as first-loss risk capital. Disproportionally large capital injection requirements are another risk to euro area tax payers in rescues of thinly capitalized banks. There is consequently across the euro area a large degree of interdependence between the financial solidity of large domestic banking systems and national government solvency.

The bank large ownership of government debt in the euro area presents a particularly intractable concern. Euro area (and other) banks are under the Basle Agreements not required to set aside any risk capital to offset any future losses on government bond holdings. Sovereign bonds have by definition been deemed "risk free". Consequently, when Greek government debt must be restructured, it will impose upon the euro area banks credit losses for which they have previously not set aside capital, and given the scale of ownership of such debt among domestic Greek banks will require that these be recapitalized with money from international donors. The same dynamic is inevitable across essentially all euro area members, as the domestic banking system will face ruinous capital losses if national sovereign debt is restructured, due to the high domestic government debt ownership.

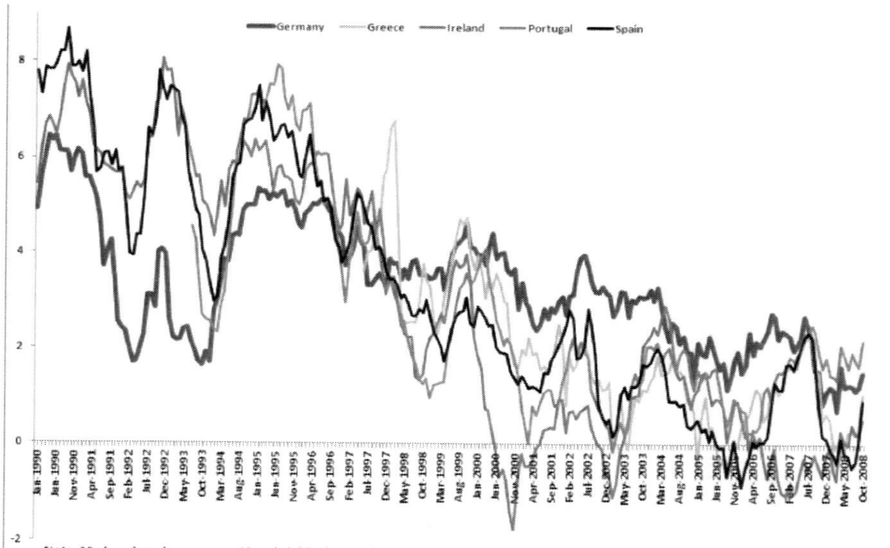

Note: 10y benchmark government bond yield subtracted annual national CPI levels 1990-1998. National HICP inflation rates from Jan 1999. *Source: Eurostat; OECD*

Figure 5. Long-term Real Interest Rates Jan 1990-Oct 2008.

Fearful that banks would require very large amounts of new equity capital, which would in many instances have to come from governments themselves and might therefore pose a challenge to some governments' own solvency, European banking regulators have been reluctant to include any potential impairment of banks' sovereign debt holdings in EU bank stress tests in 2010 and 2011. Given, however, the justified market concerns about the solvency of at least one euro area sovereign (Greece) and the potential for contagion to other euro area sovereign bond markets, stress tests that do not include the potential for losses on sovereign bonds cannot provide a credible measure of the riskiness of any euro area banking system. As long as solvency concerns exists about euro area governments, a high degree of volatility will surround the euro area banking system, which again provide a powerful feedback loop to increased investor fears about the financial stability of governments in the first place.

Table 1. Banking Systems in the Euro Area 2011

	Financial Institutions' Gross Debt (% of GDP)	Bank Leverage (Ratio of tangible assets/common equity in domestic banks)	Bank Claims on the Public Sector (Percent of GDP)
Euro Area	143	26	N/A
Belgium	112	30	23
France	151	26	17
Germany	98	32	23
Greece	22	17	28
Ireland	689	18	25
Italy	96	20	32
Portugal	61	17	24
Spain	111	19	24
United States	*94*	*12*	*8*

Source: IMF GFSR September 2011, table 1.1

Lastly, in addition to low capital levels and associated concerns, many euro area banks also suffer from substantial liquidity risks with high degrees of dependence on short-term wholesale funding from markets where access may prove ephemeral and subject to rapid changes.

Euro area governments face the challenge of rapidly having to stabilize their oversized and in the aggregate undercapitalized banking systems without having to dispend large amounts of capital themselves, as this could further jeopardize their own solvency. Further postponement today of forceful measures to stabilize the euro area banking system with new outside capital risks throwing the euro area into an accelerating credit crunch as banks de-lever and conserve their scarce capital. This would rapidly have a strongly detrimental effect on the broader growth prospects of the euro area.

Not all euro area governments are in the same situation though, as for instance the German government would quite easily be able to manage an even very large government-led recapitalization of its national banking system. However, due to the close linkages among sovereigns (and consequently their banking systems) inside the euro area and the observable presence of contagion between them, a key challenge for European policymakers will be to move expeditiously to a new system of tougher pan- European banking support, regulation and supervision. The establishment of a new set of common regulatory institutions for the European banking system will, however, due to the obvious implications potential government financial crisis support for banks have for governments' own solvency require a new level of fiscal integration in the euro area and the commensurate loss of national fiscal sovereignty. The fact that the City of London, the EU and euro area financial center, is located in the UK, which can safely be assumed to remain outside the euro area itself for the foreseeable future, further complicates this type of banking sector integration initiatives.

End Notes

[1] See Euro Area Summit Statement at http://www.consilium.europa.eu/uedocs/cmsdata/docs/pressdata/en/ec/125644.pdf.

[2] Available at http://aei.pitt.edu/1002/1/monetarywernerfinal.pdf.

[3] Available at http://aei.pitt.edu/1007/1/monetarydelors.pdf.

[4] Available at http://www.eurotreaties.com/maastrichtec.pdf.

[5] See Kirkegaard (2010) at http://www.piie.com/publications/pb/pb10-25.pdf.

[6] The actual numerical reference values to article 104c of the Maastricht Treaty are in a Protocol on the Excessive Deficit Procedure to the Treaty. Available at http://www.eurotreaties.com/maastrichtprotocols.pdf. The Maastricht Convergence Criteria for euro area membership eligibility include three additional metrics; inflation (within 1.5 percent of the three EU countries with the lowest inflation rate); long-term interest rates (within 2 percent of the three lowest interest rates in the EU); and exchange rate fluctuations (participation for two years in the ERM II narrow band of exchange rate fluctuations).

[7] See EU Council Conclusions March 23rd 2005 at http://www.consilium.europa.eu/uedocs/cmsdata/docs/pressdata/en/ec/84335.pdf.

[8] See IMF press release 11/374 at http://www.imf.org/external/np/sec/pr/2011/pr11374.htm and IMF press release 11/330 at http://www.imf.org/external/np/sec/pr/2011/pr11330.htm.

[9] See speech by ECB vice-president Vitor Constancio for a precise definition and discussion at http://www.ecb.int/press/key/date/2011/html/sp111010.en.html.

[10] Article 123 in the EU Treaty states "*Overdraft facilities or any other type of credit facility with the European Central Bank or with the central banks of the Member States (hereinafter referred to as 'national central banks') in favour of Union institutions, bodies, offices or agencies, central governments, regional, local or other public authorities, other bodies*

governed by public law, or public undertakings of Member States shall be prohibited, as shall the purchase directly from them by the European Central Bank or national central banks of debt instruments."

[11] As discussed above, with the vast majority of European citizens still self-identifying as citizens of their respective countries (rather than the euro area), a pooling of all the national sovereign debts of the euro area into a single debt instruments – similar to what Alexander Hamilton achieved for the U.S. states' war debts in 1790– is not a realistic political option in Europe at this point. Another critical political difference is that unlike the war debts incurred by U.S. states during the Revolutionary War, the outstanding debts of individual euro area members have not been incurred in order to achieve a "common cause". The political narrative of seeing such debts "honored in common" by all euro area members consequently does not exist.

[12] http://www.ecb.i nt/ecb/lega l/pdf/fxac08115enc_002.pdf.

[13] http://www.federalreserve.gov/aboutthefed/section31.htm

[14] Full text of ECB letter to Silvio Berlusconi at http://www.corriere.it/economia/11settembre29/trichetdraghiinglese304a5f1e-ea59-11e0-ae06- 4da866778017.shtml?fr=correlati.

[15] See Duval and Elmeskov (2005) for an in-depth analysis at http://www.ecb.int/pu b/pdf/scpwps/ecbwp596.pdf.

[16] It can be seen in figure 4 how peripheral deficits have declined substantially since 2008. This, however, can be mostly related to the severe economic contractions experienced in the euro area periphery, which has temporarily caused import levels to collapse.

[17] I shall in this testimony not discuss the option of member leaving the euro area. I will refrain from this for three main reasons; first of all, I consider the costs of any country leaving the euro area as catastrophically high for the country in question, irrespective of whether it is Greece or Germany. Secondly, it is clear from the political announcements of all EU leaders that the departure of any country from the euro area will not be tolerated (such a departure could prove to have a very serious contagion effect). And thirdly, as under the current EU Treaty, the departure from the euro area is legally undefined and thus presumed impossible.

[18] See the Nyberg Report at http://www.bankinginquiry.gov.ie/Documents/Misjuding%20Risk%20-%20Causes%20of%20the%20Systemic%20Banking%20Crisis%20in%20Ireland.pdf.

INDEX

#

20th century, 54

A

access, 36, 58, 94, 100, 107, 108, 139, 144, 145, 149
accounting, 25, 105
adjustment, 7, 53, 68, 71, 77, 81, 83, 85, 90, 93, 98, 106, 109
Afghanistan, 26, 104
agencies, 46, 140, 151
aging population, 124
Alexander Hamilton, 62, 151
anxiety, 8
appetite, 81, 85, 105
appropriations, 24, 34
Arab countries, 104
architects, 52
Argentina, 92
arrest, 83
Asia, 71
assessment, 48, 85
assets, 20, 39, 44, 47, 80, 89, 91, 92, 104, 146
Austria, 31, 83
authorities, 11, 30, 45, 59, 66, 108, 112, 116, 142, 151
authority, 7, 57, 134

B

background information, 132
backlash, 16
bail, 66, 88, 100, 131, 143
balance of payments, 106
balance sheet, 49, 73, 84, 94, 95, 114, 116
balanced budget, 9, 13, 14
Balkans, 26
ban, 66, 103
bank debt, 91, 105, 108
bank holding companies, 48
Bank of Canada, 41, 127, 128
Bank of England, 41, 127, 128
banking, ix, x, 1, 2, 3, 4, 5, 10, 14, 19, 36, 38, 39, 45, 51, 64, 66, 67, 80, 81, 105, 106, 107, 108, 121, 124, 129, 131, 133, 146, 147, 148, 149, 150
banking sector, ix, 3, 81, 146, 150
bankruptcy, 19
bargaining, 60, 61
barriers, 7, 118, 119
base, 83, 85, 95
basis points, 46, 68, 113
Belgium, 31, 56, 83, 121, 135
beneficiaries, 143
benefits, 16, 55, 66, 79, 84, 124, 143
benign, 89

bond market, 63, 65, 66, 76, 78, 139, 143, 148
bondholders, 10, 16, 39, 108
bonds, x, 2, 5, 8, 10, 15, 18, 53, 60, 63, 66, 67, 68, 77, 78, 79, 83, 84, 91, 92, 94, 99, 100, 108, 120, 123, 147, 148
borrowers, 70
Brazil, 64, 71
breakdown, 73
breathing, 83, 85
Bretton Woods system, 55, 133
Britain, 90, 119
Budget Committee, xi, 51, 75, 97
budget cuts, 14, 81, 87
budget deficit, 4, 9, 11, 13, 37, 76, 81, 82, 83, 84, 86, 121, 122, 124, 125, 126, 127
business environment, 38
businesses, 45, 46, 105, 113, 114, 120, 138

C

cabinet, 107
capital adequacy, 48
capital flight, 5, 15, 88
capital flows, 72, 106
capital markets, 5, 97, 124
capital outflow, 82
cash, x, 2, 10, 11, 30, 87
census, 28
central bank, 13, 21, 22, 41, 46, 49, 59, 60, 63, 66, 73, 84, 86, 87, 104, 113, 114, 115, 116, 117, 127, 139, 140, 141, 151
challenges, ix, 1, 3, 4, 14, 25, 48, 104, 105, 106, 112, 125, 127
chicken, 61, 67
China, 12, 32, 53, 54, 64, 65, 71, 122, 131
citizens, 87, 88, 98, 151
city, 94, 150
classes, 53
close relationships, 115
collaboration, 59
collateral, 11, 15, 19, 39, 44, 47, 61, 66, 108, 112
collateral damage, 61
collective bargaining, 145
commercial, 46, 85
commercial bank, 46, 85
commodity, 119
competition, 7
competitive advantage, 120
competitiveness, 9, 14, 16, 36, 38, 45, 51, 54, 81, 82, 84, 86, 95, 105, 106, 107, 108, 125, 126, 129, 133, 145
complement, 56
complexity, 77, 129
compliance, 107
concrete thinking, 133
conference, 65, 87, 94
conflict, 70, 99
congress, vii, ix, 1, 2, 3, 4, 18, 22, 23, 24, 33, 59, 71, 72, 124, 140
consensus, 70
consolidation, 13, 37, 38, 39, 69, 108, 130, 143, 145
constitution, 69
consumers, 45, 138
contradiction, 52
controversial, 31
convention, 31
convergence, 13, 56, 57, 135, 137, 144
convergence criteria, 56, 57, 135, 137
cooperation, 4, 20, 25, 26, 115
coordination, 17, 52, 55, 57, 108, 112, 133, 134, 137
copper, 119
correlation, 143
cost, 40, 44, 46, 65, 75, 82, 99, 112, 113, 116, 139, 143
costs of production, 17
Council of Ministers, 77, 78
counterterrorism, 26
credit market, 66
credit rating, 11, 19
creditor nation, 86, 90
creditors, 5, 31, 53, 66, 71, 78, 79, 84, 86, 88, 99, 107, 120, 139
creditworthiness, 83, 122
crises, 6, 14, 51, 52, 54, 58, 86, 87, 93, 106, 129, 133
criticism, 12, 21

cultural differences, 125
culture, 119
currency, 7, 15, 21, 22, 30, 51, 54, 55, 57, 58, 60, 88, 90, 91, 92, 93, 97, 99, 101, 106, 112, 114, 115, 118, 119, 120, 125, 134, 137, 138, 139, 140, 141, 144, 145, 146
current account, 51, 68, 71, 133, 144
current account deficit, 51, 68, 71, 133
current account surplus, 71
Cyprus, 31
Czech Republic, 11

D

danger, 76, 87, 100, 137
debt crisis, ix, 1, 3, 21, 24, 129, 132
debtors, 61, 73, 88, 120
debts, 7, 16, 44, 62, 77, 80, 81, 83, 84, 85, 86, 89, 90, 106, 111, 120, 139, 151
decision makers, 61
deficit, 37, 56, 57, 72, 81, 122, 123, 127, 135, 137, 140, 145
deflation, 101
denial, 58
Denmark, 118
deposits, 88
depreciation, 20, 84
depth, 151
designers, 134
Deutsche Mark, 54
devaluation, 81, 82, 83, 101
developed countries, 23
developing countries, 25
development assistance, 25
diplomacy, 100
direct action, 132
direct taxes, 134
disaster, 52, 53, 142
disbursement, 23
disclosure, 39
dislocation, 130
distortions, 124
distribution, 63
divergence, 56, 135
Dodd-Frank Wall Street Reform and Consumer Protection Act, 24
domestic economy, 132
domestic factors, 146
donors, 104, 147
draft, 11, 24, 107
drawing, 46, 114, 115, 124
dream, 89
dynamism, 38

E

early warning, 11
earning power, 123
earnings, 95, 115
economic activity, 112, 113, 118, 126
Economic and Monetary Union, 52
economic competitiveness, 7, 14, 118
economic crisis, ix, 1, 59, 61, 62, 118, 132
economic development, 46
economic downturn, 16, 39, 88
economic fundamentals, 57, 58, 64, 137, 138
economic growth, 13, 14, 16, 36, 38, 39, 40, 42, 45, 67, 119, 122, 140, 145, 146
economic growth rate, 146
economic incentives, 25
economic institutions, 69
economic integration, 17, 54
economic problem, 21, 117, 122
economic reform, x, 2, 13, 23, 38, 39
economic relations, 2, 33, 104
economic theory, 137
economic union, 52, 56, 134
Ecuador, 120
elected leaders, 60
election, 17, 89
emergency, 100, 142
emerging markets, 20, 65, 71
employees, 125
employers, 125
employment, 108
EMU, 52, 55, 56, 133, 134
encouragement, 36
energy, 104, 107

enforcement, 11, 45, 57, 137
engineering, 67, 68
environment, 63, 95
equity, 47, 80, 123, 131, 146, 148
erosion, 38
Estonia, 31, 93
EU enlargement, 25
Eurasia, 31
European Banking Authority (EBA), 6, 39
European Central Bank, x, 2, 7, 36, 44, 52, 55, 76, 99, 108, 112, 113, 122, 128, 131, 134, 151
European Commission, 9, 11, 25, 34
European Community, 55, 133
European integration, 4, 12, 14, 17, 52, 70
European Monetary System, 55, 133
European Monetary Union, 36, 106
European Parliament, 65
European policy, 4, 44, 45, 55, 58, 98, 133, 138, 142, 145, 150
European System of Central Banks, 73
Eurozone governments, ix, x, 2, 3, 5, 6, 8, 9, 23
evidence, 81, 89
evolution, 52
exchange rate, 7, 21, 29, 30, 31, 33, 46, 54, 68, 81, 83, 90, 93, 114, 119, 133, 150
exercise, 8, 48, 69, 71, 140
expenditures, 37
exporters, 71
export-led growth, 15, 54
exports, 2, 7, 16, 17, 20, 40, 44, 69, 95, 104, 109, 112, 119, 125, 126, 145
exposure, 2, 4, 18, 19, 22, 23, 40, 47, 105
expulsion, 61
external financing, 70, 81

F

factories, 125
families, 105
FDI, 105
FDIC, 75
fear, 6, 10, 16, 23, 82, 92, 100, 139
fears, 16, 37, 40, 52, 92, 148
federal funds, 116
federal government, 59, 127
Federal Reserve, vii, xi, 20, 21, 22, 43, 45, 46, 48, 49, 59, 94, 111, 113, 114, 115, 116, 117, 140
fencing, 142
financial commitments, 12, 24
financial condition, 41, 44, 104
financial crisis, x, 2, 5, 21, 40, 41, 46, 47, 58, 72, 107, 109, 137, 138, 140, 141, 145, 150
financial firms, 47
financial institutions, 2, 6, 18, 19, 44, 45, 46, 47, 48, 70, 91, 93, 95, 111, 112, 113, 114, 116, 130, 131, 146
financial markets, 7, 10, 15, 22, 40, 44, 46, 57, 58, 59, 72, 89, 93, 105, 111, 112, 113, 114, 116, 124, 130, 137, 139, 141
financial resources, 16, 40, 41, 132
financial sector, 38, 47, 76, 107
financial stability, 15, 33, 35, 42, 131, 133, 143, 148
financial support, 8, 12, 13, 36, 38, 130, 139, 143, 145
financial system, 18, 19, 20, 36, 37, 40, 49, 92, 105, 112, 116, 127
Finland, 31
fires, 39
firewalls, 45
fiscal deficit, 31, 98
fiscal policy, 106
fiscal surpluses, 37
fixed rate, 116
flaws, 57, 58, 138
flexibility, 9, 10, 16, 57, 108, 137
fluctuations, 55, 73, 114, 133, 150
force, 67, 78, 87, 100, 101, 106, 139
forecasting, 6
foreign assistance, 25
foreign banks, 46
foreign companies, 94
foreign exchange, 64, 71
foreign investment, 58, 70
foreign policy, 4, 25, 70
foundations, 108

France, 6, 7, 12, 13, 17, 31, 40, 54, 55, 57, 58, 80, 83, 86, 87, 89, 94, 98, 121, 122, 134, 137
funding, 36, 39, 40, 44, 45, 46, 48, 49, 66, 80, 93, 104, 108, 109, 112, 115, 116, 122, 149
funds, 3, 5, 8, 12, 19, 23, 24, 25, 36, 40, 45, 47, 71, 78, 83, 85, 86, 88, 91, 93, 114, 116

G

GDP, 6, 9, 10, 18, 24, 36, 37, 40, 68, 79, 81, 83, 84, 85, 86, 88, 91, 94, 95, 97, 108, 118, 121, 122, 124, 126, 127, 136, 139, 144, 146
Germany, 6, 7, 12, 13, 14, 15, 31, 37, 40, 52, 53, 54, 55, 57, 61, 62, 67, 68, 69, 70, 80, 82, 84, 87, 88, 89, 90, 92, 94, 95, 97, 98, 99, 100, 101, 106, 120, 121, 122, 134, 137, 144, 146, 151
global economy, ix, 4, 21, 44, 47, 90, 92, 94, 104, 109, 126, 130, 133
global markets, 46
global security, 25
GNP, 81, 94
goods and services, 18, 40, 44, 68, 104
governance, 9, 11, 17, 52, 104, 107, 108
government budget, 9, 11, 125
government revenues, 140
government spending, 37, 122, 123
governments, ix, x, 2, 3, 4, 5, 6, 7, 8, 11, 13, 14, 15, 16, 17, 18, 23, 31, 36, 37, 38, 39, 40, 53, 57, 60, 61, 64, 65, 66, 73, 75, 76, 98, 99, 112, 122, 138, 140, 142, 146, 148, 149, 151
gravity, 106
Great Depression, 90
Great Recession, 52, 54, 58
greed, 113
Greeks, 101, 121
growth, x, 2, 6, 14, 16, 17, 20, 35, 36, 38, 39, 40, 44, 54, 67, 68, 70, 81, 82, 83, 86, 90, 93, 104, 105, 107, 108, 109, 110, 111, 137, 146, 149
growth rate, 20
guidance, 55

H

Hamilton, Alexander, 62, 151
health, 53, 110
hedging, 130
history, 52, 68, 69, 98
Hong Kong, 71
host, 125
house, x, xi, 3, 4, 24, 31, 35, 43, 117
housing, 37

I

identification, 134
imbalances, x, 1, 2, 4, 6, 11, 16, 31, 45, 51, 104, 106, 133, 144, 145
import substitution, 125
imports, 20, 58, 103, 120, 145
in transition, 104
income, 24, 78, 124
independence, 13, 59, 140, 141, 142
individuals, 79
industries, 119
industry, 82, 119, 124
inflation, 22, 73, 89, 91, 100, 101, 120, 150
initiation, 55, 133, 142
institutional change, 76
institutional reforms, 69
institutions, x, 2, 8, 12, 13, 15, 19, 21, 36, 44, 47, 48, 52, 58, 59, 60, 62, 69, 111, 112, 113, 114, 115, 133, 138, 139, 140, 150, 151
integration, 18, 31, 53, 54, 55, 63, 68, 69, 106, 118, 132, 150
interdependence, 147
interest rates, 5, 37, 39, 57, 58, 68, 72, 73, 78, 81, 83, 84, 86, 91, 92, 93, 98, 100, 108, 114, 119, 122, 123, 137, 138, 139, 140, 146, 150
international competitiveness, 54, 119, 127

International Monetary Fund (IMF), x, 2, 3, 4, 5, 6, 8, 9, 11, 22, 23, 24, 30, 31, 32, 33, 34, 36, 37, 39, 41, 42, 63, 64, 65, 66, 67, 70, 71, 72, 73, 78, 79, 84, 85, 94, 95, 106, 109, 121, 122, 130, 131, 132, 138, 139, 143, 146, 150
intervention, 14, 79, 100
investment, 18, 19, 20, 86, 104, 107, 112, 131
investments, 91, 131, 145
investors, ix, 3, 10, 20, 44, 57, 63, 66, 77, 78, 81, 83, 90, 91, 92, 100, 116, 123, 131, 138, 139, 140, 141
Iran, 26, 103
Ireland, x, 2, 4, 5, 8, 9, 19, 22, 23, 30, 31, 37, 38, 41, 51, 60, 64, 70, 79, 80, 81, 82, 86, 88, 94, 95, 106, 119, 121, 122, 130, 133, 139, 143, 146
isolation, 129
issues, ix, 4, 7, 14, 18, 20, 21, 48, 62, 118, 138
Italy, x, 2, 4, 5, 6, 8, 9, 16, 17, 19, 23, 31, 37, 40, 56, 60, 61, 62, 63, 64, 65, 67, 68, 70, 73, 79, 80, 81, 82, 87, 88, 95, 107, 119, 121, 122, 125, 130, 135, 139, 140, 143

J

Japan, 41, 46, 71, 113, 122, 127, 128
job creation, 54
jurisdiction, 132

K

kill, 38
Korea, 33, 71

L

labor market, 7, 9, 38, 68, 144, 145
lack of confidence, 52
Latin America, 90
Latvia, 68, 93
law enforcement, 26
laws, 38, 78, 119, 125
lead, 14, 21, 54, 76, 85, 89, 130, 132, 145
leadership, ix, 3, 54, 89, 107, 109, 142
learning, 123
legality, 18
legislation, 3, 11, 17, 23, 24, 71
lender of last resort, 13, 141
lending, 6, 7, 8, 14, 22, 23, 39, 46, 66, 83, 112, 115, 127
liberalization, 107
light, 4
liquid assets, 30
liquidity, x, 2, 10, 15, 21, 39, 47, 49, 64, 66, 73, 76, 104, 105, 107, 108, 113, 114, 116, 121, 127, 149
Lithuania, 93
loans, 9, 10, 24, 46, 61, 63, 66, 70, 73, 79, 91, 112, 113
locus, 69

M

Maastricht Treaty, 55, 56, 57, 73, 121, 134, 135, 137, 150
magnitude, 70, 127
majority, 17, 41, 47, 48, 63, 89, 104, 143, 151
management, 61, 64, 140
market access, 82
marketplace, 124
materials, 49, 114, 116
matter, 53, 127, 131
Medicare, 127
membership, 7, 17, 56, 73, 135, 150
merchandise, 105
Mexico, 64
Microsoft, 95
Middle East, 25, 71
military, 61
mission, 26
mold, 140
momentum, 40, 54
monetary policy, 7, 18, 65, 76, 97

monetary union, 17, 37, 38, 45, 52, 55, 56, 57, 69, 97, 99, 106, 118, 133, 134, 137
money markets, 22, 46, 113
money supply, 22
moral hazard, 12, 15, 18, 53, 57, 60, 137
multimedia, 34

N

national debt, 89, 97
national security, 70
NATO, 26
negative effects, 125, 126
negotiating, 5, 10
Netherlands, 31, 106, 121
North Africa, 25
Norway, 118

O

Obama, 4, 21, 22, 24, 33, 99
Obama Administration, 4, 21, 22, 24
obstacles, 8, 15, 145
offenders, 100
officials, 3, 12, 13, 14, 18, 23, 25, 59, 92, 141, 142
oil, 55, 71, 103, 133
operations, x, 2, 10, 14, 15, 22, 39, 44, 94, 115
opinion polls, 89
opportunities, 20, 104
Organization for Economic Cooperation and Development (OECD), 6, 28, 32, 139
overlap, 8, 131
oversight, 23, 69
ownership, 131, 147

P

pain, 98
Panama, 120
parity, 55, 134
Parliament, 65, 100
participants, 46, 64, 105, 135
peace, 26
performers, 18
permit, 60, 106, 114
petroleum, 104
plaque, 146
playing, 25, 88
pleasure, 129
Poland, 84
policy, x, 1, 2, 4, 7, 8, 13, 15, 16, 21, 48, 54, 57, 59, 62, 65, 68, 72, 76, 94, 112, 119, 125, 139, 146
policy issues, 125
policy makers, 139
policy options, 146
policy responses, 8, 16, 21
policymakers, 13, 14, 25, 31, 38, 129
political crisis, 69
political leaders, 54, 56, 57, 61, 76, 89, 92, 98, 134, 137
political legitimacy, 63
political opposition, 82
politics, 52, 77, 86, 87, 90
popular support, 89
population, 92, 118, 124
portfolio, 80
Portugal, x, 2, 4, 5, 6, 8, 9, 19, 22, 23, 30, 31, 37, 38, 41, 61, 64, 70, 79, 80, 81, 82, 86, 106, 119, 122, 130, 139, 143
precedent, 15, 140, 142
president, 12, 21, 33, 55, 87, 106, 107, 134, 150
President Obama, 21, 33
price stability, 13
principles, 13
private banks, x, 2, 66
private sector, 7, 10, 31, 33, 37, 38, 53, 78
privatization, 38
probability, 87, 90, 131
production costs, 7
profitability, 124
project, 4, 14, 52, 53, 54, 55, 68, 70, 71, 134
prosperity, 25, 98
protection, 32, 47, 80, 115, 130
public debt, 5, 16, 24, 31, 37, 122
public finance, 5, 57, 107, 137

public opinion, 32
public pension, 124
public sector, 145
public support, 17

Q

quotas, 24, 71

R

radar, 66
reactions, 21, 52, 85
real estate, 145, 146
real time, 59
real wage, 10
reality, 55, 56, 63, 72, 81, 90, 134, 135
reasoning, 100
recession, ix, x, 1, 3, 6, 37, 45, 48, 70, 75, 82, 90, 95, 101, 122, 124, 126
recognition, 123
recovery, ix, 1, 35, 40, 93, 104, 109, 110, 113
reform, 9, 13, 18, 24, 32, 35, 38, 40, 43, 56, 59, 60, 61, 62, 69, 72, 87, 88, 100, 107, 108, 109, 117, 130, 139, 142, 146
reforms, x, 2, 9, 10, 11, 13, 16, 24, 25, 36, 37, 38, 39, 40, 41, 68, 71, 72, 87, 107, 108, 142, 144, 146
regional policy, 61
regulations, 95, 134, 144
repair, 38, 107
requirements, 15, 39, 45, 47, 131, 145, 147
reserve currency, 58
reserves, 30, 64, 70, 71, 78, 140
resilience, 47, 49, 110
resistance, 8, 121
resolution, 40, 45, 60, 69, 109, 132
resources, 8, 12, 22, 23, 24, 41, 53, 60, 63, 65, 67, 70, 71, 73, 106, 109, 122, 130, 131, 143
response, 7, 8, 10, 12, 13, 14, 16, 17, 21, 30, 41, 43, 59, 65, 109, 111
restoration, 141
restrictions, 141
restructuring, x, 2, 10, 38, 77, 85, 86, 90, 107, 125, 130, 143
retail, 107
retained earnings, 85
retirement, 124
retirement age, 124
revenue, 81
rights, 71, 78
risk, 21, 39, 46, 47, 57, 62, 75, 76, 77, 79, 80, 81, 82, 83, 84, 87, 88, 89, 90, 91, 92, 93, 94, 97, 100, 105, 113, 114, 115, 123, 124, 127, 130, 131, 137, 140, 147
risks, x, 2, 3, 16, 18, 20, 39, 47, 48, 53, 76, 79, 84, 86, 87, 90, 103, 104, 106, 113, 147, 149
root, 15, 107
roots, 134
ruble, 92
rules, 11, 45, 56, 57, 62, 69, 95, 98, 112, 134, 137, 138, 143
Russia, 64, 71

S

safe haven, 94
sanctions, 100
savings, 38, 91, 105, 107, 127
savings banks, 38, 107
savings rate, 127
scope, 12, 57, 76, 85, 129
secondary markets, x, 2, 8, 10, 15, 39
securities, 11, 15, 112
security, 25, 54, 115
senate, xi, 3, 4, 19, 24, 31, 33, 51, 75, 97, 103, 111, 129
Senate Foreign Relations Committee, xi, 129
sequencing, 65
services, 28, 104, 118, 119, 124
shape, 20
shareholders, 64, 73
shock, 20, 55, 132, 134
shores, 35
short-term interest rate, 91

showing, 79
signs, 137
silver, 119
Singapore, 71
single currency, 31, 55, 134, 143
Slovakia, 31
social costs, 93
Social Security, 127
society, 79, 91, 93
solidarity, ix, 3, 12, 98, 101
solution, 18, 38, 58, 67, 77, 99, 109, 110, 129, 142
sovereign bonds, x, 2, 6, 15, 63, 66, 67, 77, 78, 108, 148
sovereignty, 13, 62, 99, 138, 150
Soviet Union, 92
Spain, x, 2, 4, 5, 6, 8, 9, 16, 19, 23, 31, 32, 37, 38, 40, 60, 61, 63, 64, 65, 67, 70, 80, 81, 82, 95, 106, 107, 119, 122, 139, 140, 143
speculation, 5
speech, 79, 94, 150
spending, 3, 7, 9, 25, 39, 63, 72, 81, 86, 98, 99, 100, 101, 126, 127
spillovers, 116, 130
stability, ix, 1, 3, 4, 22, 23, 25, 26, 85, 86, 100, 103, 109, 130, 131
Stability and Growth Pact (SGP), 57, 137
stabilization, 48, 84, 104, 131
standard of living, 98
state, 25, 62, 63, 93, 106
states, ix, 3, 7, 11, 12, 13, 17, 31, 36, 38, 55, 56, 62, 80, 108, 134, 138, 140, 141, 144, 151
statistics, 33
statutes, 131
stimulus, 59, 72, 126
stock, 19, 44, 79, 81, 83
stock price, 44
stress, 20, 22, 39, 48, 66, 95, 105, 106, 123, 148
stress test, 20, 22, 39, 123, 148
structural changes, 68
structural reforms, 9, 16, 45, 60, 67, 87, 108, 144, 145
structure, 7, 77, 93
style, 101
substitution, 125
supervision, 11, 150
supervisors, 47
Supreme Court, 120, 140
surplus, 11, 54, 64, 65, 68, 72, 79, 106, 122, 145, 146
surveillance, 11, 17
survival, 54, 67, 84, 91
sustainability, 5, 36, 44, 76, 95, 104, 107, 108, 109, 111, 118, 130, 137, 139
Sweden, 118
Switzerland, 46, 113, 118
symptoms, 106

T

tactics, 59
target, 56, 81, 135
tax base, 95
tax collection, 125
tax increase, 9
tax policy, 86
tax system, 119, 127
taxation, 63
taxes, 39, 62, 101, 134
taxpayers, 63, 115, 117, 131
tension, 45
tensions, 18, 36, 39, 46, 108, 119
time frame, 56
total costs, 85
total revenue, 37
trade, x, 1, 2, 3, 6, 12, 16, 18, 20, 28, 31, 33, 48, 54, 71, 91, 112, 118, 131
trade deficit, 7
trading partners, 40, 95, 145
transactions, 49, 114, 115, 116
transcripts, 33
transformation, 77
transformations, 25
transmission, 65
transport, 104, 107
treasury, vii, x, 3, 21, 24, 32, 35, 59, 62
treasury bills, 62

Treasury Secretary, vii, x, 21, 35
treatment, 77
triggers, 87

U

U.S. economy, 4, 18, 44, 103, 113, 116, 117, 126
U.S. policy, 4, 117, 132
U.S. Treasury, xi, 11
unemployment rate, 126
uniform, 121
unions, 125, 145
unit of account, 119, 120
united, vii, xi, 2, 3, 4, 11, 18, 20, 21, 22, 23, 25, 26, 33, 35, 40, 41, 43, 44, 46, 48, 58, 59, 62, 63, 69, 71, 72, 90, 103, 104, 105, 107, 109, 112, 113, 118, 119, 120, 121, 122, 124, 125, 126, 127, 130, 132
United Kingdom (UK), 11, 12, 46, 62, 90, 113, 118, 121, 132, 150
United States, vii, xi, 2, 3, 4, 12, 18, 20, 21, 22, 23, 25, 26, 33, 35, 40, 41, 43, 44, 46, 48, 58, 59, 62, 63, 69, 71, 72, 103, 104, 105, 107, 109, 112, 113, 118, 119, 120, 122, 124, 125, 126, 127, 130, 132
unpopular austerity reforms, x, 2

V

vehicles, 131
venture capital, 125
veto, 72, 100, 121
vision, 54, 65, 138
volatility, 53, 81, 129, 130, 142, 143, 146, 148
vote, 72
voters, 17, 121
voting, 24, 71
vulnerability, 7

W

wage level, 145
wages, 17, 81, 82, 90, 98
war, 41, 90, 109, 151
Washington, 31, 73
weakness, 72, 121
wealth, 92, 105, 109
web, 116
websites, 49, 116
welfare, 124, 125
welfare state, 124
White House, 33, 94
wholesale, 149
World Bank, 33
worry, 14, 59, 127

Y

yield, 79, 92
young people, 104